"The use of object-mail, grabbers, and freemiums plays a role in almost every direct-mail campaign I develop for my private clients as well as for my own use, and Travis Lee at 3D Mail Results is my go-to guy for these items and for fresh ideas. I have brought in Travis and his team for projects, referred clients to him, and turned to him time and again for the right items at the right price. You'd be foolish not to use 3D Mail Results as your preferred resource, as I do."
DAN S. KENNEDY, DIRECT-RESPONSE LEGEND

"All of our members know that not only do I like 3D Mail a lot, but I use them a lot. And there is no mystery as to why I use them. It's not because I want to make my mailing more complex and complicated. It's only because I want my mailing to have a better response, and that's exactly what they do. 3D Mail does a lot of great things, but the biggest thing it does, which is the only thing our members should even be paying attention to is, it increases response. The return on your investment will be much, much higher than the cost of it, so it just always pays for itself."
BILL GLAZER, WORD RENOWNED MARKETING STRATEGIES AND BEST-SELLING AUTHOR

"I doubled the response I was getting to my best control package using 3D Mail. Based on my results I have endorsed 3D Mail to my members. I would recommend using 3D Mail to anyone looking to increase their sales and more importantly, their profits."
RORY FATT, RESTAURANT MARKETING SYSTEMS

"With your 3D Mail pieces, I've experienced as much as a quadrupling in response rate over "flat" letters and postcards. There's just nothing like dimensional mail...it's like being a kid again, ripping open your mail to see what the surprise is inside! You've helped to make sending dimensional mail easy. Thanks to you, my prospects now have three piles of mail: A-pile, B-pile, and "3-D Pile".
DR. CHRISTOPHER BOMAN, ADVANCED DENTISTRY

"These 3D pieces make a huge difference in our income. People do not expect to see them in their mailbox, especially from an industrial sales guy. The letters that 3D Mail Results provide me let me get to look like the hero because I look like I'm a great copy-writer, but I'm not. I just put my name on it; insert their products and send it to my clients. Money comes in the mail."
WALTER BERGERON, SERIAL ENTREPENEUR AND BEST-SELLING AUTHOR

"We got an $18.00 return for every dollar that we invested in a 3D mailing using their Bank Bag program. Every time we do something with 3D Mail Results, it produces multiple returns on our investment. We've been using 3-D Mail Results for about 4 years. Every time we work with them we generate multiple returns on our investment. They are great folks to work with. We consider them to be marketing partners who are integral to our success in direct response."
STEVE CLARK, NEW SCHOOL SELLING

How small businesses can make
huge profits using direct mail

THE SIMPLE
3-STEP PROCESS
THAT ENSURES DIRECT MAIL
SUCCESS

Travis Lee

This publication is designed to provide accurate and authoritative information regarding the subject matter covered. It is sold with the understanding that the publisher is not engaged in rendering legal, accounting, or other professional services. If legal advice or other expert assistance is required, the services of a competent professional person should be sought.

For more information, contact:

3D Mail Results
Travis Lee
PO Box 2356
Buckley, WA 98321

Discounts are available for bulk purchases.
Email info@3dmailresults.com

Contents

CHAPTER 4

The Simple 3-Step Process That Ensures Direct Mail Success

Direct mail can provide a great return on your marketing dollar, if done correctly. But too many businesses go at it haphazardly, with no strategy or game plan in place before they start. They simply 'wing it' and hope for the best. That's a bad business strategy for anything, but it can be multiplied and worsened with direct mail.

However, there is a tried and true 3-pronged direct mail system that, when followed correctly, can return huge dollars to any business, any size, in any industry.

In this book, Travis Lee (co-founder and president of 3D Mail) reveals the 3-pronged "plan of attack" that virtually ensures direct mail success. While this 3-pronged direct mail system is nothing new (it's been around since the late 1800's), it's rarely spoken about, except for in the most exclusive direct mail circles.

If you're considering the use of direct mail, this book will save you thousands of dollars and hundreds of hours in mistakes, errors and frustration. Don't play blind archery. Don't do this by yourself. Uncover the secrets used by elite direct mail professionals throughout the world to multiply their sales and income.

What to Expect in This Book And How to Best Profit by It

You are smarter than the average bear in the woods.

Congratulations.

Many business owners foolishly decry direct mail as dead. Old. Out of touch. They sneer and call it "snail mail." They hopelessly lust after the cheap and easy, and mostly focus on "online." But as Mark Twain famously once said, "The report of my death has been greatly exaggerated."

Many businesses, both great and small, are STILL reaping the benefits of paper and ink, real mail, sent via the real post office, to millions of consumer and business mailboxes every day.

Facts About Direct Mail:

> Direct Mail ad spend was 44.5 BILLION in 2014***, more than broadcast and cable television, radio, newspaper, and magazine. Only the catchall of "Internet" has more, at $49.5 billion**
> 50% of people say they pay more attention to postal mail than email*
> 60% of people say they enjoy checking their mailbox*
> 65% say they receive too much email*
> 98% retrieve mail every day, 77% read and sort the same day*
> 59% of business owners prefer printed resources to online resources*

*Epsilon channel preference study, 2014
** IAB/PwC Internet Ad Revenue Report, 2014
*** Winterberry Group Analysis, 2013

A common denominator for businesses that are struggling or failing is the absence of a direct-mail system that works and steady investment in it.

On the next page you'll see a list of the top 50 mailers as measured by volume. **What do these companies know that you may not?**

NAME	INDUTRY	LIST MANAGER
1. American Express Co.	Financial Services	Does Not Rent
2. Chase Bank	Financial Services	Does Not Rent
3. Comcast Corp.	Telecom/Cable	Does Not Rent
4. Capital One	Financial Services	Does Not Rent
5. AAA	Clubs/Associations	Does Not Rent
6. Citibank	Financial Services	Does Not Rent
7. AT&T Communications	Telecom	Does Not Rent
8. GEICO Direct	Insurance	Does Not Rent
9. Verizon Communications	Telecom	Does Not Rent
10. Discover Financial Services	Financial Services	Does Not Rent
11. L.L.Bean	Catalog	Does Not Rent
12. Macy's	Retail	Does Not rent
13. Oriental Trading Company	Catalog	Infogroup Targeting Solutions
14. Omaha Steaks	Foods	SMS Marketing Services
15. J.C. Penney	Retail	Does Not Rent
16. Lands' End	Catalog	Infogroup Targeting Services
17. March of Dimes	Nonprofit	Infogroup Targeting Services
18. State Farm Insurance Cos.	Insurance	Does Not Rent
19. Bank of America	Financial Services	Does Not Rent
20. Kohl's	Catalog	Does Not Rent
21. Wells Fargo & Co.	Financial Services	Does Not Rent
22. Cox Communications Inc.	Cable	Does Not Rent
23. The DIRECTV Group, Inc.	Cable	Does Not Rent
24. Pottery Barn	Catalog	SMS Marketing Services
25. ASPCA	Nonprofit	American List Counsel
26. Pep Boys	Automotive	Does Not Rent
27. ASPE Technology	Seminars/Training	Does Not Rent
28. Salvation Army	Nonprofit	Does Not Rent
29. Costco Wholesale	Retail	Does Not Rent
30. Allstate Insurance Co.	Insurance	Does Not Rent
31. Viking River Cruises, Inc.	Travel	Does Not Rent
32. Daedalus Books & Music	Catalog	SMS Marketing Services
33. Dell Inc.	Technology	Does Not Rent
34. 4Imprint Inc.	Catalog	MeritDirect
35. Vermont Country Store	Catalog	Belardi/Ostroy
36. AARP	Clubs/Associations	Does Not Rent
37. St. Jude Children's Research Hospital	Nonprofit	Does Not Rent
38. Old Pueblo Traders	Nonprofit	Does Not Rent
39. Planned Parenthood Federation of America, Inc.	Nonprofit	Lake Group Media, Inc.
40. Globe Life And Accident Insurance Co.	Insurance	Does Not Rent
41. Home Decorators Collection	Home Furnishings	Belardi/Ostroy
42. Bed Bath & Beyond Inc.	Retail	Does Not Rent
43. BJ's Wholesale Club	Retail	Does Not Rent
44. Crate & Barrel	Catalog	SMS Marketing Services
45. Victoria's Secret Direct	Catalog	Does Not Rent
46. Mutual of Omaha	Insurance	Does Not Rent
47. Athleta Corp.	Catalog	Belardi/Ostroy
48. Wounded Warrior Project	Nonprofit	National Fundraising Lists
49. Nordstrom	Retail	Does Not Rent
50. Independence Blue Cross	Insurance	Does Not Rent

As I said, you're smarter than the average bear. Proof that you are reading this book about a subject that most business operators are not interested in. But you are here, at least open-minded about doing some different things to find, keep, and profit from using direct mail.

How to End Income Uncertainty

Having a very predictable income should be a vital goal. Income uncertainty plagues most business owners and often perpetuates an underlying tension and unhappiness at home with spouse and family. It's why even quite successful owners often half-joke about the people close to them still hope they'll "settle down and get a good job." Income uncertainty or unpredictable revenue also injects underlying anxiety into the staff of the business and gets in the way of their top performance. When you stabilize the income, you gain authority with those around you. People have confidence in you. There's less complaining. You and they can focus on forward achievement rather than worrying. One of the best cures for income uncertainty is improvements in and systemization of your direct mail marketing.

Very predictable income makes business more pleasurable, easier to manage, and much more valuable when the day comes to exit by sale. When properly presented to a potential buyer of a company, predictable income has a higher multiple value than does unpredictable income. Recurring revenue has an even higher multiple. One of the things an owner sells when he sells his company is projected future earnings at a discount. The more certain those future earnings appear to be, the less he must discount and the more money he exits the scene with.

When you finish this book, three things should have occurred: one, you have a far richer and better understanding of the financial importance of direct mail. Two, you have all the elements needed to assemble systems for profiting using direct mail. Three, you are highly motivated and determined to get those systems up and running. Arguably, presuming some of the first and third are already present, the second of these is most important. And the key word is systems.

I teach that all wealth is the product of systems. Henry Ford's wealth and the Ford family dynasty wealth he set in motion is not the product of any invention of combustible engine or automobile. It is thanks to the system of the assembly-line for manufacturing and the system of franchised auto dealers. You can peel back the curtain of any successful company in any field and make similar discoveries.

This book will reveal the systems need to consistently, predictively, and profitably generate income via direct mail.

Michael Gerber popularized the idea of systems in business in his groundbreaking, bestselling book, *The E-Myth*. Preceding Gerber, credit is deservedly given to Peter Drucker. But most business owners apply this direction to only management, to business operations, not to marketing or sales, and almost never to direct mail. If you do so, you will gain significant competitive advantage, you may gain price and profit elasticity, and you can build a stronger and more valuable company!

One last point: you will see and hear stories, case studies, and campaigns from many different businesses in this book. Each did an outstanding job in profiting with direct mail in very different businesses. DO NOT make the common, dumb, mistake of quickly deciding their examples can't help you because your business is different. All businesses can make huge sums of money using direct mail. Don't be myopic. Second, most breakthroughs in one type of business come about by borrowing ideas from other, seemingly unrelated businesses. Don't be Amish. Be curious and imaginative.

CHAPTER 1

Direct Mail Success Secret #1: Choosing the Right List For Maximum Success

It's been my experience that proper list selection makes up half the battle in direct mail. You may quibble and say, "Well, it's only 40% or it's only 42.7%," or some other number like that. But the fact is that list selection is by far the most important aspect of direct mail success.

You can have the greatest copy written by the greatest copywriter (dead or alive) to write your copy; if it goes to the wrong list, you're never going to have success. However, with careful list selection, even an average copywriter can get anywhere from good to amazing results if the right list is targeted.

I've found that the topic of mailing lists is something that most marketers don't know a whole lot about. We're going to dive deep into lists and you'll see how you can use mailing lists successfully in your direct mail campaigns.

In this section, I'm going to give you five battle-tested mailing list strategies that will ensure you have the most success with direct mail and ultimately, make more sales.

Whether you sell B2B or B2C, there are only two kinds of lists available:

- Your in-house list of prospects and clients, both past and present.
- Rented or purchased, commercially available list.

We will start with your in-house lists; however, the focus will be on purchased and rented lists. I find that most of my clients really have no clue about what's available with rented and purchased lists.

Within your in-house list, there are three types of people: active buyers, non-buyers and prospects, inactive/lost customers.

In-House List

Active buyers

These are the people who buy from you, who are currently buying from you; they have a purchasing history with you. And when they need what you have, there's a pretty good chance that they're going to call up and get it from you.

Virtually every business owner fails to fully mine the gold in his own customer list while running around everywhere, hunting for the next new customer. Most people look everywhere for an opportunity, happiness, etc. except under their own feet which are, quite frankly, where you're most likely to find it. A lot of people completely undervalue and under-appreciate their customer's ability and willingness to buy. What are the things you can do to stimulate purchases or stimulate activity from your current clients or customers?

The first thing that you can do is to make more offers to them more often. Something else you can do is offer more products or services. Now, this doesn't have to be your products or services. Take a Realtor for example:

You know that if you're a realtor and your customers purchase a home, they have one thing in common, and that is, they own a house. That's the one thing that they have in common. What are the things that they would need that you could offer? For example, if they've bought a house, you can work with a painter and get a referral fee for interior/exterior painting. What about furniture? What about home improvements? That's just one niche but you can offer anything that compliments what you already know about your customers. Don't be limited in the fact that, "Okay, I have products A, B, and C and that's the only thing I can offer these people and get a monetary payback from it." That's simply not the case.

You can reward frequent purchases. Obviously, we are all part of rewards programs —some are better than others. One I really like is a company called Royaltyrewards.com. It keeps tracks of points, it offers members the point value that equals the dollar value that they can use on a monthly, quarterly or yearly basis.

You can reward high volume purchases with dollars off or bundled services. You can incentivize greater usage, you can communicate frequently with information and education. Those who've been on my mailing list for any amount of time can attest that I give all kinds of frequent information and education.

For those who get my monthly newsletter, there's always a section called "Take a Break." There's Sudoku, word search, funny business-related memes, etc. It's not all BUY NOW calls to action. That means you need to communicate consistently and frequently. You build relationships with regular communication, not haphazard communication.

If you're going to do an e-mail tip, make sure it is either weekly, bi-weekly, or monthly and stick to it. If you're going to be using a hard copy, i.e. sent-in-the-mail newsletter, you should do it every month. Don't do it every quarter, don't do it every other month, do it every month. Again, the frequency and the consistency are most important when communicating with your current and active clients.

In addition, identify and focus like a laser beam on your hyper-responsive people. Almost every business has hyper-responsive people who will buy, purchase, or invest in almost anything you put out there. What you can do is keep a list of those people; whether it's just old-fashioned Excel spreadsheets or you have some sort of whiz-bang CRM system that can tell you who these people are.

If you've got that short list ready to go when you need or want a quick influx of cash, that's the way to go. Here's the bottom line: A buyer is always a buyer, therefore, it's infinitely easier and always more profitable to work at increasing the purchasing of your satisfied customers than it is to go out and add new ones. Even If you don't get anything else out of this book, get it drilled into your head that the best place for you to go mining, is in the current clients and patients and members you already have.

Non-Buyers/Leads/Prospects.

Every business has these people in its system. I'll call them *unconverted leads* from here on. But this is a great segment of your list to make joint venture or affiliate offers as we discussed with our realtor example. Could you even partner with a competitor here? Chances are that many of these people still have a need for a similar solution that you offer but just not your specific solution.

For example, you're a painter who specializes in high-end homes with top-quality paints and service but have unconverted leads from price conscious consumers. Maybe, they own rental properties and they're not necessarily in the high-end part of town and they're not really concerned with the paint looking the best but are instead, more concerned about the price. You can work with another painter who does work with those "not so high-quality consumers." That's just a splendid example of one way where you can leverage your current non-buyers and turn them into paying people.

Here's another example:

If you're a chiropractor and you have unconverted leads for your practice, maybe you can refer them to an acupuncturist. Then you're getting part of the action. There's a big portion of your list that didn't take any action so offer them your solution or make a complementary offer. Again, you don't have to be the one that fulfills the product or service, but you should be the one getting some sort of payment to monetize your leads.

I'll use the realtor example once more. In that example, we knew that they had bought a house. So, we knew that they had certain requirements that all the new homeowners required. Now, here with these non-buyers, these are people who have inquired or asked for more information. They haven't purchased so they're not quite good as those people yet, but we do know they all have something in common. What they had in common was a need, a want, a desire, an itch to scratch for your solution or what it is that you offer. Again, don't be limited in your thinking in how you can monetize your non-buyers.

5

Inactive/Lost Customers

These are people who have purchased from you but have not been back in an ordinary amount of time. That time varies from business to business. In some industries, the timeframe is an "industry norm." For example, every six months, you need to go see your dentist —that's what they have you believe anyway. You change your oil every 3 months or 3,000 miles.

 Most business completely underuse their Lost and Inactive Cutomers. For a comprehensive, FREE Training on how to profit by targeting your Inactive/Lost customers visit Lost.3DMailResults.com

For some of you, you're going to have to find the sweet spot. For example, a lunch-time diner in a busy downtown setting, for your regular clients, it might be a few days or weeks. Bob comes in for lunch every Tuesday. And then, Bob doesn't come in Tuesday this week; Bob's lost. What do we do to get Bob back?

Maybe you have a retail store that sells running shoes, your "sweet spot" may be every six months.

For a high-end jeweler, maybe it's every 18 to 36 months. If he's married, he's probably getting her SOMETHING every third birthday or anniversary. May as well be from you!

For our businesses, and we mainly live in the B2B world, the magic number seems to be anywhere from six to 12 months. That number varies but you need to try and find the sweet spot for your business.

Rented/Purchased Available Lists

There are two types here and we're going to talk about both in great depth.

- Response-based list
- Compiled list

Response-based list

A response-based list are lists of people who have bought a specific product from a company. The "in-house buyers" list of the company that made the initial sale.

My Company, 3D Mail Results, can supply you with response based lists of all kinds, those mentioned in this book and 1,000's of others. For details call (360) 761-7382 or info@3DMailResults.com

For example, *Harry & David™* who sell gift baskets of fruits and cheeses and meats, etc. *Omaha Steaks™* that sell meats prepared meals. *Sharper Image™* and their fun electronic gadgets and doodads and stuff like that. They all make their buyers list available for purchase. Have you ever wondered why after you order ANYTHING via direct mail; a wine club, a vacation, a magazine... you end up getting more and more offers for related items... BINGO! You name was sold to a competing or complimentary company. That's a response-based list **based on purchases**.

There's also a response-based list **based on inquiries**. These are people who inquired about something but didn't make a purchase. For example, maybe you called about the

Sleep Number™ Bed or a *Sun Setter Awning™*, but you didn't purchase, you'd be on their "inquiry" list. You could rent the in-house list of Sharper Image based on their purchases or you could be renting the in-house list of Sharper Image based on their inquiries.

Could you make your list available for purchase? It's certainly something that many businesses do. It's the dirty secret of most of these direct response companies. Big companies like *Harry & David™*, *Omaha Steaks™*, *Sharper Image™* etc. make a lot of money on selling their own products and services, but where they make a whole lot of money is renting the list of the purchase history of their customers. That is the essence of what a purchased or rented list is.

Compiled list

This is where most marketers start because they think that's the only thing available. Here we'll talk about the good and bad of both the response list and the compiled list.

In general, with the compiled list, we can get more information about the specific person on the list, but we don't know if they were a responder or a buyer. We can get age, income, and other demographic information based on warranty cards, public, or government records, credit bureaus, surveys and all those contest forms people fill out.

Here's another dirty little secret. As soon as you enter a contest for *Publisher's Clearinghouse™*, they have a record of you; who you are and what you do when you fill out a mini-survey. They compile that information and then, they sell that information. They sell that information to companies that we call, *"list compilers."* These are companies that you may recognize from their names like Axiom, Excelsior, or Experian.

Axiom, Excelsior, and Experian are the three big players in the compiled list world, essentially the credit score companies of the world. They compile all that data and then give you a credit score. That credit score is only worth so much money. But what is also worth a whole bunch of money is you filling out demographic information on warranty cards or public records and government records.

Looking for a complied list including new movers, new borrowers, and saturation lists? Call my team for detail, (360) 761-7382 or info@3DMailResults.com

For example, we can find out the property taxes that you pay on a home or a piece of property. Then, of course, from there, we can extrapolate what we believe that home to be worth and we can figure out quickly what 'John Doe's' home is worth. When you register for a wedding, it is compiled. *Pottery Barn™*,for example is on our 50-largest mailers list in the preface of this book.

What happens when you get on their list? Well, they're probably selling your name as a soon-to-be-married or recently married but that's a little different. These are the things you're going to see with the likes of Info-USA and their neighbors to the north, Info-Canada. They're going to sell you, primarily, what's called a compiled list.

That's where we get prospects of "between 50 and 65," with a certain amount of household income and a certain amount of net worth and two teenagers in the home still. That's a compiled list. Generally, we can get more demographic data with compiled lists. However, I'm going to show you some examples where that's not the case.

What about compiled versus response?

What is the difference? A compiled list is a group of data pulled together. But, as I already mentioned, we don't know if it's responsive at all. A response-based list means that they bought or inquired, but we may not know the income or marital status. I prefer a response-based list, but we can't always get a response-based list for your exact avatar, perfect client, or perfect prospect.

Data Cards

Data cards tell you the make-up of your list. They tell you exactly what is on the list that you inquired about, so they can vary slightly from what you're seeing in the samples.

We'll go through a handful of examples. This first example is a B2B compiled list.

Report Info

Name:	Travis Lee at 3D Mail Results

Count Info

Search ID:	15018HAV-854
Search Description:	15018HAV-854 DN7 08/06/15
Run:	August 06, 2015
Modified:	August 06, 2015
Search Notes:	Geography:
	Radius:
	Granularity: ZIP+CRRT
	98004~Miles:20~Same State:1
	Selections:
	SIC Codes:
	Custom Computer Programming Services
	Exact Sales Volume:
	0 to 250000
	Employee Size:
	1 - 4 employees
	Phones & Contacts:
	One per Company/Phone:
	One per phone
	DPV Physical Address Quality Status:
	Delivery Point Validated
	Telephones & Contacts:
	100% Telephones + Contacts Where Available
	Only records with ZIP+4:
	Only Records with ZIP+4

Let's start from the top and work our way down. You see business database, multi-use with contacts, titles and phone, list count report.

Search Notes: When it comes to geography, we can select by state, city, zip code, county, or a radius surrounding a fixed point. In this case, we did a radius, zip code, 20 miles around 98004 and the same state equals one —which means we went 20 miles in and around zip code 98004 and it had to be in the same state.

Next is SIC Code, which is how we search for the type of businesses, in this case, "custom computer programming services."

11

Next, we have exact sale volume, we want it under $250,000. It could have been $250 million, it could have been $2 million, anything we want.

Next, employee size of one to four. Phone and contacts, we want one per company and one per phone. DPV is the physical address quality status, we always use the highest status possible. Again, whether you get a list from us or not, we're going to say that this is the highest delivery. This is delivery point validated. What that means is the address is validated and has an extremely high likelihood of delivery (95%+).

Below that we have telephones and contacts; we only want 100% telephone and contacts available. In this case, we only wanted 100% telephone numbers. In the B2B world, this does stunt it.

If we didn't choose this, we would certainly get more names but it's not as big of a deal in the B2B world. In the B2C world, that's going to cut our number down considerably because any list will be scrubbed against the national do-not-call list. It's been my experience, as a big general rule of thumb, if you want 100% phone numbers in the consumer world, you're only going to get between 8% and 20% of the total list size.

Let's look at a consumer database list count report:

1	Consumer Database - List Count Report	
2	**Report Info**	
3	Name:	Travis Lee at 3D Mail Results
4	**Count Info**	
5	Search ID:	15018HAV-855
6	Search Description:	15018HAV-855 AMH 08/06/15
7	Run:	August 06, 2015
8	Modified:	August 06, 2015
	Search Notes:	State: AK, AZ, CA, HI, ID, MT, NV, OR, UT, WA, WY Demographics Age: Age 18-19, Age 20-21, Age 22-23, Age 24-25, Age 26-27, Age 28-29, Age 30-31, Age 32-33, Age 34-35, Age 36-37, Age 38-39, Age 40-41, Age 42-43, Age 44-45, Age 46-47, Age 48-49, Age 50-51, Age 52-53, Age 54-55 Address Type Indicator: Undetermined, Single Family Dwelling, Apartment with Unit #, Apartment without Unit#, Rural Route Household Health: Or logic, Allergies in Household Gender: Female Age & Gender of Children: Or logic, Age 0-2 Male, Age 3-5 Male, Age 0-2 Female, Age 3-5 Female, Age 0-2 Unknown Gender, Age 3-5 Unknown Gender Phones & Mail:

In this one, we selected the western states: Alaska, Arizona, California, Hawaii, Idaho, etc. We did demographics: there's the age, the address type indicator. This one's a little different, the address type indicator is undetermined, so we don't know what kind of dwelling it is (house, apartment, condo, etc.).

13

We look and see household health. We wanted to know if someone had allergies in the household, were female, and they had kids between the ages of zero and five.

Here's another data card. This is the data card of the membership of *Entrepreneur Magazine* (next page). You'll see here that there's 1.4 million in the total universe. In the last 24 months, there's been 727,000 members; last 12 months, there's been 424,000; in the last six months, 197,000.

SEGMENTS

1,452,980	Total Universe/Base Rate	$120.00/M
727,605	Last 24 Month Hotline	
424,344	Last 12 Month Hotline	+ $7.00/M
197,883	Last 6 Month Hotline	+ $11.00/M
92,429	Last 3 Month Hotline	+ $15.00/M
25,535	Last 30 Day Hotline	+ $21.00/M
	Fundraiser Rate	$75.00/M
	Catalog Rate	$95.00/M
443,281	Expires	$100.00/M

DESCRIPTION

Entrepreneur delivers distinctive content for the independent thinkers, builders, and leaders who are driving the growth of business across the country. It serves as the primary source of business owners seeking to grow and expand their businesses as well as professionals seeking to become entrepreneurs.

The definitive guide to the diverse challenges of business ownership, Entrepreneur equips business owners and managers with the critical information they use to grow their businesses. Every issue is as inspirational as it is informational to motivate readers in addition to providing need-to-know material for how to succeed.

Reach a vast audience eager to learn more, do more, and get more from their businesses. These business owners seek information, tools, and resources, for new, established, and growing businesses. They wish to attain higher levels of success or get started on the road to self-employment. These professionals and decision makers are affluent, educated, and passionate about business. Entrepreneur understands what is wanted and needed and provides informative means and the guidance needed to conquer the daily challenges in business.

Entrepreneur.com is the #1 website for self-employed/C-Level execs/owners and in the top 3% of websites for business decision makers.

Entrepreneur ranked #1 selling Business Magazine on Newsstand for 4 years! These entrepreneurs need guidance, support, and solutions. They attend conferences, seminars, and webinars as well as subscribe to many publications. They are quick to acquire anything that will give them an edge from the latest handhelds to financing to software.

Entrepreneur subscribers own and purchase property, belong to private-club memberships, and buy art and collectibles.

Individual Demographics:
Median Age 41
$467,000 Average net worth
$941,337 Median household value
78% Own residence
47% Millionaire households
81% Use Investment Advisor
50% Have a membership at a private club
44% Own 2 or more properties
34% Buy art or collectibles

DATE
CONFIRMED   10/23/2013

UNIT OF SALE
$59.00

GENDER
59% MALE
41% FEMALE

MEDIA
Direct mail sold

ADDRESSING

CHESHIRE LABELS	NO CHARGE
EMAIL	$75.00/F
P/S LABELS	$10.00/M

ADDITIONAL CHARGES

12 Month Hotline	$7.00/M
3 Month Hotline	$15.00/M
6 Month Hotline	$11.00/M
Business Address	$8.00/M
Demographic	$12.00/M
Gender/Sex	$10.00/M
Geo/Geographical	$10.00/M
Home Address	$8.00/M
Lifestyle	$12.00/M
Paid	$10.00/M
Phone Number	$26.00/M
Source	$10.00/M
Zip	$10.00/M

MINIMUM ORDER
7,500
$350.00 MINIMUM PAYMENT

NET NAME POLICY

Net Name is allowed	85%
Min Qty	50,000

Going down the right side you see your pricing and other information; 59% male, 41% female. Let's look to the lef column for the description – general information and individual demographic. Not all data cards are going to have this information. The median average age is 41, $467,000 in average net worth, $941,000 median household value, 78%

15

owned residences, so they give you more of that. Let's look at another one.

This next one is from the Sharper Image and this is their enhanced master file. You see the audience profile; the catalog offers one-of-a-kind gifts across multiple categories. You'll see here 802,000 total universes, 15,597 bought one month, 38,000 bought a three month and so on and so forth.

SHARPER IMAGE
Enhanced Masterfile

The Sharper Image catalog and website offers high-ticket electronics, personal care, fitness equipment, unique gifts, home furnishings, housewares, jewelry and travel accessories. In addition to traditional enhancement overlay data, Sharper Image is also offering Co-Op enhanced data.

SEGMENTS		PRICE
802,344	TOTAL UNIVERSE / BASE RATE	$120.00/M
15,597	1 Month Buyers	+ $37.00/M
38,634	3 Month Buyers	+ $32.00/M
74,491	6 Month Buyers	+ $17.00/M
257,341	12 Month Buyers	+ $12.00/M
	Fundraisers	$70.00/M
	Publishers	$70.00/M

ID NUMBER

NextMark Manager	406176
UNIVERSE	
802,344	
LIST TYPE	
Consumer	

DESCRIPTION

Audience Profile
The Sharper Image catalog offers one-of-a-kind gifts across multiple categories. From hi-tech electronics, gadgets, air purifiers, sleep solutions, home furnishings, travel essentials, and the latest and greatest toys & games. These avid, highly-responsive consumers have purchased from the Sharper Image catalog and website. In addition to traditional enhancement overlay data, Sharper Image is also offering Co-Op enhanced data.

sharperimage.com

12 Month Product Select - $15/M

Accessories	29,840
Apparel	10,871
Auto	19,241
Bathroom	49,547
Bedroom	38,290
Electronics	58,451
Games / Toys	27,971
Gift Card	711
Gift Certificate	553
Health Management	5,833
Holiday	3,165
Home Comfort	32,492
Home Furnishings	8,011
Home Maintenance	2,614
Home / Office	21,134
Kitchen / Entertaining	24,206
Massage	26,252
Nostalgia	1,925
Outdoor	20,579
Pain Relief	7,087
Pet	2,621
Travel	13,948

SOURCE
Direct mail sold

LIST MAINTENANCE

Counts through	06/30/2015
Last update	08/03/2015
Next update	08/31/2015

SELECTS

$100 + BUYERS	42.00/M
$150 + BUYERS	52.00/M
$25 + BUYERS	17.00/M
$30 + BUYERS	19.00/M
$50 + BUYERS	22.00/M
$75 + BUYERS	32.00/M
1 MONTH HOTLINE	37.00/M
12 MONTH HOTLINE	12.00/M
12 Month Product Select	15.00/M
3 MONTH HOTLINE	32.00/M
6 MONTH HOTLINE	17.00/M
AGE	11.00/M
AILMENTS	16.00/M
BUYER ACTIVITY	16.00/M
BUYER PRODUCT	16.00/M
GENDER	8.00/M
INCOME SELECT	11.00/M
MAIL ORDER BUYER	16.00/M
PRESENCE OF CHILDREN	11.00/M
PRODUCT SELECTS	
SCF	11.00/M
STATE	11.00/M
ZIP TAPE	11.00/M

GEOGRAPHY
USA

UNIT OF SALE INFORMATION

Average:	$135

GENDER PROFILE

Male:	34%
Female:	57%

AVERAGE INCOME

Dollar:	$90,000

16

AP

Amerimark
Herrington
J Peterman Company
Wintersilks

EP

Harry and David
Omaha Creative Group Incorporated

Edu

Sky & Telescope

FR

California State Automobile Association
Disabled American Veterans
Humane Society
MD Anderson Cancer Research Center
Museum of Modern Art
National Museum of the US Army
Rescue Missions Consortium
Robbins Kersten Direct
St Jude Children's Research Hospital
Zoo Consortium

Finance

Discover Financial Services

GH

Company Store

On the right, you see "Source, direct mail sold." That means these people were sold via direct mail. That could be good for you so if you're going to use direct mail and you want to target people, what could be better than a list of people who had bought via direct mail already.

Then, we can sort by dollar value of the purchase, how recently they've purchased, their age; we can get ailments, in fact. That's what we mean by enhanced master file, this has all this extra stuff here. There are 12-month products select so if they bought accessories, apparel, auto, bathroom, bedroom, electronics, so you can see the people who just bought those kinds of purchases.

This data card has what's called USAGE, so these are companies that have bought this list already and have mailed to it. Some names you may recognize; J. Peterman Company, Harry & David, Omaha Creative Group, The Humane Society, St. Jude's Children Hospital, Heartland of America, and Office Depot are companies who had bought this list or some portion of this list.

17

I'm going to show you two different lists that we found for a client and you'll see the differences between each one. This first one is doctors who are heavy investors, with their home addresses. This is much smaller than the Sharper Image example.

This is a response-based list of both buyers and inquiries, and you'll see our total universe is 743,000, and this is the doctor's home postal address. This one's a little different. We wanted a specific profession so it's kind of merging a business list because we wanted a list of doctors, but then we wanted their home addresses.

Page

SEGMENTS

743,229	Total Universe/Base Rate	$85.00/M
743,229	Doctors Who are Heavy Investors	$85.00/M
236,482	At Home Address	$85.00/M
19,481	With Home Telephone Number (DNC Suppressed)	
$105.00/M		
506,388	At Office Address	$85.00/M
492,196	With Office Telephone Number	$105.00/M
650,125	By Medical Area	$85.00/M
539,344	OPT-IN EMAIL ADDRESS	$210.00/M

DESCRIPTION

Doctors who are heavy investors in securities and/or tax shelters. They have invested or inquired to invest.

Doctors at home postal address, state of MN, Active investors in last 12 months = 6,435   Price for this selection is $92 per thousand with 5,000 minimum order

DATE
UPDATED   06/20/2014
CONFIRMED   06/20/2014

UNIT OF SALE
$10,000.00 Average Investment amount

GENDER
90% MALE
10% FEMALE

MEDIA
Opt-in e-mail, Direct response, Compiled lists

ADDRESSING

E-MAIL / FTP	$50.00/F
CD ROM	$50.00/F
P.S. LABELS	$10.00/M
BAR CODING	$10.00/M
CARRIER RT. SORT	$10.00/M
EMAIL - PERSONALIZATION	$25.00/M
EMAIL - DEPLOYMENT	$25.00/M

ADDITIONAL CHARGES

AGE	NO CHARGE
GENDER	$5.00/M
INCOME SELECT	NO CHARGE
NET WORTH	$10.00/M
PHONE NUMBER	$20.00/M
ZIP/SCF/COUNTY/STATE	$7.00/M

MINIMUM ORDER
5,000

NET NAME POLICY
Net Name is allowed

This data card won't have as many choices as Sharper Image. You'll see the description and the segments. On the right-hand side, 90% male, 10% female, then we have the

18

additional charges on the right. We can get age at no additional charge. We can get the gender, income, net worth, phone number, etc. The minimum order is 5,000.

Now, let's go look at the other list that we could choose from for this client. Another list of medical healthcare professionals who invest. This one has a little more information (next page):

SEGMENTS

6,625,425	Total Universe/Base Rate	$70.00/M
2,318,899	With Telephone Numbers	~$15.00/M
515,547	With DNC Scrubbed Telephones	$15.00/M
1,306,979	With Email Addresses	$125.00/M
2,471,505	Active Investors	$20.00/M
186,040	Property Investors w/2+ Properties	$20.00/M

DESCRIPTION

Doctors only at home address, State of MN = 14,845
Pricing for this selection is $80 per thousand with
3,000 minimum order (one time use) Available for
unlimited use for $150/M

These affluent healthcare professionals have a high net worth
and/or have made mutual fund, stock/bond and or real estate
investments.

Additional Charges:
Expiration Date @ $5/M
Income Producing Assets @ $15/M
Nurse Type @ $5/M
State of Licensure @ $5/M

Chezhire Labels @ N/C

50+ Telephone numbers

DNC scrubbed monthly.

NCOA'd every 6 weeks.

PROFILE

INCOME RANGE	$5.00/M	
$30,000 - $34,999		376,155
$35,000 - $59,999		265,365
$60,000 - $64,999		358,213
$65,000 - $74,999		568,939
$75,000 - $99,999		1,224,955
$100,000 - $149,999		1,248,559
$150,000 - $174,999		233,276
$175,000 - $199,999		121,315
$200,000 - $249,999		236,691
$250,000 +		930,260
NET WORTH	$15.00/M	
$200,000 - $99,999		236,915
$200,000 - $249,999		960,244
$250,000 - $499,999		932,299
$500,000 - $749,999		296,872
Investment Type	$10.00/M	
Life Insurance Investments		1,930,215
Mutual Funds Investments		1,271,210
Real Estate Investments		1,633,936
Stocks/Bonds Investments		2,164,548
# of Properties Owned	$15.00/M	
2 Properties		111,897
3 Properties		46,414
4-5 Properties		23,613
6 or More Properties		14,112

DATE

UPDATED	06/20/2014
CONFIRMED	06/20/2014

MEDIA

Direct response, Government records, Opt-in
e-mail, Compiled lists

ADDRESSING

CD ROM	$25.00/F
EMAIL	$25.00/F
P/S LABELS	$8.00/M

ADDITIONAL CHARGES

AGE	$5.00/M
AGE OF CHILDREN	$5.00/M
CONTRIBUTORS/DONORS	$10.00/M
GEOGRAPHY - ZIP, COUNTY, SCF, ETC	$5.00
CREDIT CARD BUYERS	$10.00/M
DWELLING TYPE	$5.00/M
ETHNICITY	$15.00/M
GENDER OF CHILD	$5.00/M
GENDER/SEX	$5.00/M
HEALTH & FITNESS	$10.00/M
HOME OWNER	$5.00/M
INCOME RANGE	$5.00/M
LENGTH OF RESIDENCE	$5.00/M
LIFESTYLE INTERESTS	$10.00/M
MAIL ORDER BUYERS	$5.00/M
MARITAL STATUS	$5.00/M
NET WORTH	$15.00/M
NUMBER OF CHILDREN	$5.00/M
PHONE NUMBER	$15.00/M
PRESENCE OF CHILDREN	$5.00/M
RELIGION	$15.00/M
SPORTS INTEREST	$10.00/M
STATE	NO CHARGE
STATE OF LICENSURE	$5.00/M
TRAVEL INTERESTS	$10.00/M
Investment Type	$10.00/M
# of Properties Owned	$15.00/M

MINIMUM ORDER

3,000
$210.00 MINIMUM PAYMENT

NET NAME POLICY

Net Name is allowed	85%
Min Qty	50,000
Run Charges	$8.00/M

You see 6.6 million in the total universe. And again, doctors only at home address staying in Minnesota. On the right, you'll see the additional charges: age, age of children, contribution donors, dwelling type, income, there's various kinds.

And then here's the description. These are affluent healthcare professionals, have a high net worth and/or have made mutual funds, stock/bond, or real estate investments. You then see the income range, the net worth ranges, the

20

investment types. Minimum order is only 3,000 so significantly less than the other cards we've reviewed.

We're going to look at one more data card, so you can see some of the differences. Always start with the description.

---

mplete Medical's Ailments, Illnesses and Medical Conditions   09/24/2014   M221569|NM221569

EGMENTS

112,391,600	Total Universe/Base Rate	$150.00/M
94,884,598	Total with Telephone Numbers	+ $25.00/M
14,166,209	Total with E-mail Addresses	$225.00/M

DESCRIPTION

illions of survey respondents have indicated individuals in heir households suffer from various ailments, illnesses, and ditions. This comprehensive file is selectable by hundreds of types of ailments, over-the-counter medications and rescription medications, as well as numerous household emographics including age, income, gender, marital status, so much more.

his is an ideal file for marketers of pharmaceutical and over-the-counter medication, along with distributors of medical devices and aides designed to help these consumers. This is also a strong file for those marketing magazines, credit cards, self-help, and much more.

See why we are the source for Consumer Ailments, Illnesses, and Medical Conditions:
* NCOA'd regularly and again the day your file is delivered ... guaranteed!
* Telephone numbers are DNC scrubbed every 30 days ... guaranteed!
* Numerous household demographics & lifestyle selections available to help you target your ideal audience!

PROFILE

AILMENT	NO CHARGE	
Acid Reflux	370,295	
Acne	2,671,256	
Actinic Keratosis	4,107	
Aging	60,833	
Alzheimers	1,130,606	
Anemia	31,840	
Angina	165,247	
Arteriosclerosis	2,951	
Arthritis	3,403,277	
Arthritis-Rheumatoid	2,352,207	
Asthma	4,372,158	
Asthma - Child	180,755	
Athletes foot	102,757	
Bad Breath	44,697	
Bedwetting	304,231	
Bladder Control	1,583,093	
Blindness/Visual Impairment	4,575,247	
Blood Clots	294	
Blood Disorder	430,656	
Body Odor	17,933	
Bowel Problems	26,026	
Broken Bone	1,238	
Calcium Deficiency	23,905	
Cancer	1,863,409	
Cancer - Breast	471,063	
Cancer - Kidney	3,735	
Cancer - Lung	16,165	
Cancer - Other	17,227	
Cancer - Prostate	17,192	
Cancer - Seeking Alternative Treatments	6,962	
Canker Sores	11,475	
Cardiovascular Disease	3,680	
Cataracts	20,111	
Cellulite	45,999	
Cerebral Palsy	3,556	
Chronic Bronchitis	480,683	

DATE

UPDATED	08/29/2014
CONFIRMED	08/29/2014

MEDIA
Compiled lists, Direct response

ADDRESSING

CD ROM	$25.00/F
EMAIL	$25.00/F
P/S LABELS	$8.00/M

ADDITIONAL CHARGES

AGE	$10.00/M
GENDER/SEX	$10.00/M
LIFESTYLE INTERESTS	$10.00/M
MARITAL STATUS	$10.00/M
PHONE NUMBER	$25.00/M
STATE	NO CHARGE
GEOGRAPHY - STATE, ZIP, COUNTY, ETC.	$5.00/M
AILMENT	NO CHARGE
INCOME	$10.00/M
PRESENCE OF CHILDREN	$10.00/M
EDUCATION	$10.00/M
CREDIT CARD USER	$10.00/M
HOMEOWNER	$10.00/M

MINIMUM ORDER
3,000
$525.00 MINIMUM PAYMENT

NET NAME POLICY

Net Name is allowed	85%
Min Qty	50,000
Run Charges	$8.00/M

"Millions of survey respondents have indicated individuals in their household suffer from various ailments, illnesses, and addictions. This comprehensive file is searchable by hundreds of types of ailments, over-the-counter medications, prescription medications, as well."

This is a little bit different in that this is a compiled list because these people filled out survey data. They don't have purchase data on this, but they have indicated that they or someone in their home has one of these ailments.

Next, we look at the dates in the upper right and see this was updated in August of 2014. Looking down the right we can get age, gender, lifestyle interests, marital status, phone number, the ailment, the income, the presence of children or not.

So, if you had a solution for one of these ailments, this is something you could obviously consider and investigate. Or if you have a product or service that would complement one of these. For example, let's say you're a handyman and you wanted to get a list of people who may have issues doing work around the house. You could find those ailments and then you could market to them. That would be one way to do it.

It's Not Enough To 'Think'
You Know Your Client

If you're just starting out in your business, this next section is not going to help you very much. If that's the case I suggest you skip ahead to chapter two.

Let's say you've been in business for a while and you've got a good customer list, a good customer file of people who have done business with you before. We can do what we call a regression analysis. We upload your customer list and we profile it with over 700 different data points on 200 million consumers and we find out their age, income, hobbies, interests, where they live, so you can get a snapshot of what those customers look like as a whole.

Regression Analysis

Below is a sample regression analysis. This is for U.S. addresses only. If you are new to business or if you are not US-based, this is still useful information to know. This is something that may benefit you in the future. I'll advise that

If you have over 3,500 customers in your database, a Regression Analysis can be a very power tool. Call my team for details, (888) 250-1834 or info@3dmailresults.com

you go to a list broker in your country who can do this for you if you're from outside the United States.

These are actual customers —people who have purchased before. We get that list from you in an Excel spreadsheet and we upload it against our regression analysis software and we get this cool report here. In this report, you can see that 49.97% have at least two adults in the house. Then there's the number of children in the house. We see here that most of the clients have none and very, very few have three or more.

Further down, you can see the income range. Home value estimate looks like the state average, about 150 to 200K. We see education level, the head of household, age, etc.

With age, this is the first one we've skewed one way or the other, and as you can see, we skew way right of the average age, so obviously, these people are retired for the most· part, and if we scroll up and look at income, well, if you're retired, your income isn't necessarily very high. Doesn't make you a good or bad prospect, just that your income is low, and you may be living off retirement and as a result, your income just isn't all that high.

Now, we really know what Andrew Hooker's clients look like. What could we do with this data? We can go and buy another list of these same people! You can give this information to any list broker and they can find a list of people who match this data! What better way to find new customers than by cloning your current customers!

Profile Report - Andrew Hooker

Customer File Name	Upload Date	Match Count
S_Bauer09 Q_FedSelected_Mailing.st_Thinkomantor_PL.txt	08/24/10	1827 of 2486 names

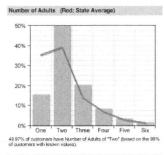

Number of Adults (Red: State Average)

49.97% of customers have Number of Adults of "Two" (based on the 99% of customers with known values).

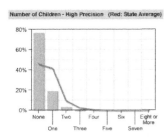

Number of Children - High Precision (Red: State Average)

Number of Children - High Precision is "None" for 76.46% of customers (based on the 80% of customers with known values).

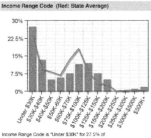

Income Range Code (Red: State Average)

Income Range Code is "Under $30K" for 27.5% of customers.

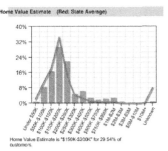

Home Value Estimate (Red: State Average)

Home Value Estimate is "$150K-$200K" for 29.54% of customers.

24

Profile Report - Andrew Hooker

Presence of Adults Female Age Bands (Red: State Average)

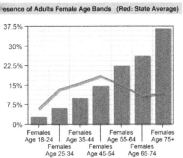

67% of customers have a Presence of Adults Female Age Bands category of Females Age 75+.

Presence of Adults Male Age Bands (Red: State Average)

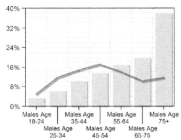

37.93% of customers have a Presence of Adults Male Age Bands category of Males Age 75+.

Discretionary Income Index Range (Red: State Average)

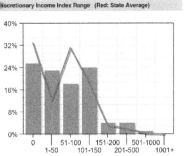

Discretionary Income Index Range is "0" for 25.57% of customers (based on the 99% of customers with known values).

Recession Sensitivity Decile (Red: State Average)

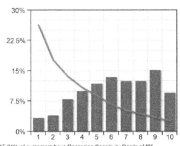

15.21% of customers have Recession Sensitivity Decile of "9" (based on the 99% of customers with known values).

Charitable Contribution Decile (Red: State Average)

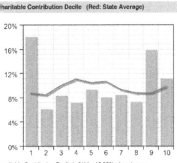

Charitable Contribution Decile is "1" for 18.08% of customers.

Net Worth (Red: State Average)

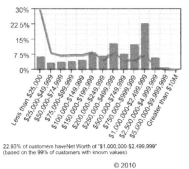

22.93% of customers have Net Worth of "$1,000,000-$2,499,999" (based on the 99% of customers with known values)

© 2010

25

Profile Report - Andrew Hooker

Household Education Level (Red: State Average)

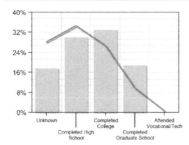

33.11% of customers have Household Education Level of "Completed College".

Head of Household Age (Red: State Average)

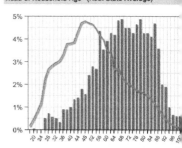

4.87% of customers have Head of Household Age of "68 or 78" (based the 98% of customers with known values).

Marital Status (Red: State Average)

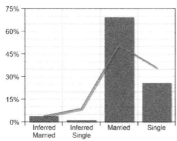

69.12% of customers have Marital Status of "Married".

Length of Residence (Red: State Average)

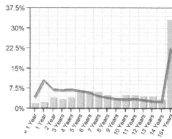

Length of Residence is "15+ Years" for 33.14% of customers (based on the 99% of customers with known values).

Head of Household Occupation (Red: State Average)

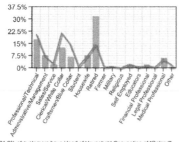

31.8% of customers have Head of Household Occupation of "Retired" (based on the 74% of customers with known values).

Home Owner Indicator (Red: State Average)

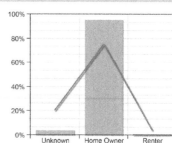

95.07% of customers have Home Owner Indicator of "Home Owner"

© 2010

26

Direct Mail Success Secret #2: Crafting A Compelling Offer For Your Products or Service

Welcome to part two of our three-part training on Direct Mail Success. This is secret number two. It is about crafting a compelling offer for your products or services.

We're going to up your copywriting and marketing ability by helping you craft offers that get response and can put money in the bank. If you can't create offers that are compelling, irresistible, and worthy to be put in front of your clients or prospects, then you are dead in the water.

What is an **"Irresistible Offer"?** Here is my definition of an irresistible offer. When you put together your offers; a marketing campaign or a sales letter, or an email, or anything else you want to present an irresistible offer.

My definition of an irresistible offer is: "what you dangle in front of your target market that gets them salivating for your product or service."

The key here is your target market. You want your offer to be precisely crafted and driven by your target market and not anybody else. That's the key here. It's not what you think an irresistible offer can be for everybody on the planet, that's not going to work. You need to think of your exact target audience and what's going to get them salivating. What's going to get them to want more of you. And what it is that you offer that will trigger an emotion with a focus on the result.

That's what we're going to do here. You know that you've hit it right when your target market says either aloud or to themselves, "I'd be a fool if I said 'No' to this."

Here is the picture I put in my mind when I'm trying to create an irresistible offer for either prospects or clients:

It's the biggest snowstorm of the year, it's February. We just got 19 inches of snow, and my direct mail piece is going to hit that day… oh, and by the way, it's Super Bowl Sunday, and my prospect's team is playing. I need to get him off the couch, move him to where I want him to go, whether that be online or to visit a store or to make him pick up the phone and make a phone call. Whatever it is, I need to get him off his couch and take an action that I want him to make.

This is the visual that I use when I do that. When you think about it in these types of terms, you're really going to up the ante when it comes to your offers that you make.

When is it appropriate to use an irresistible offer? First off, it can be used with your lead generation marketing —whether it's B2C or B2B. This is to simply get your prospect to raise their hand. It can be used for a one-step sale of your product or service. This is what you mainly see with "Madison Avenue advertising." Which basically says, here's an ad, here's our product, here's our service, buy our stuff. I'm not a huge

28

fan of this second method. Third, it can be directed at your current clients, patients or members.

Although this book is not about lead generation, we could spend hours, if not days, on that. I do want to hit on it real briefly and kind of give you an idea of what we mean by a lead generation offer and that kind of stuff. If you're going to do lead generation advertising in the hopes of finding a qualified prospect, then you need to use what we call a "lead generation magnet." That's the 'thing' that you offer as an incentive for response.

Many times, they're informational in nature, such as a report, a guide, a book, CD, or DVD, although they can be a lot of other things as well. It should be obvious that the more desirable the lead generation magnet, the better the response.

So, let's look at a few lead generation offers. On this page is an offer from, "The Survival Life." If you were a survivalist, and you were out searching for solutions, the headline "Grow enough food to feed a family of four in just

I | A | P

INTEGRITY ADVISORY PARTNERS

10 BIGGEST MISTAKES MADE IN LGBT FINANCIAL PLANNING

Comprehensive Tax and Financial Planning
Specializing in the LGBT Community

four-square feet of space, even if you don't have a yard!" would instantly jump out at you. If you're interested in survival and living off the land, this would be a great lead generation magnet.

Here's an example of a book being offered as a lead generation device. This is a client of ours, Adam Lazarus and Ryan Cole with Integrity Advisory Partners, and they've sub-niched this into a subculture or subcategory. They have a book titled *The 10 Biggest Mistakes Made in LGBT Financial Planning*. This is a book that they offer via direct mail, on their website, directed specifically at the LGBT community in their area.

Call 1-800-426-5708 to get your
FREE Catalog
and we'll send you
FREE of charge:

- **$10.00 Gift Certificate** – Use this on your first purchase
- **3 Rolls of Labels** – For your label gun. We carry almost every kind.
- **50 Merchandise Bags** – Plastic or paper. Many colors available.
- **5 Shopping Bags** – White or brown kraft. With handles.
- **15 Sign Cards** – Three different styles.
- **12 Sheets of Tissue** – Choose from 10 colors.

We pay the freight. This is totally FREE to you!
Our Guarantee
Everything at TMS is guaranteed to your complete satisfaction. If we ever let you down we will ask, "What can I do to make you happy?" In 23 years of business, we have never refused a customer's request to make them happy.

Call today to get your FREE Special Report
"Pricing To Compete With The Mass Merchandisers"

☎ 1-800-426-5708 ☎

Here's one that we used for a business we previously owned, American Retail Supply. We did this almost exclusively via direct mail for 12 years. To the left is one page of a six-page sales letter that went out to independent retail store owners. We wanted them to call in for their free catalog and other goodies; that's it.

Here's one right now that's testing very well for another business of ours. This is the mailing panel of a direct mail piece. As you can see it says

"What's the secret? How can we deliver 46,000 orders to 8,600 clients and tell every one of them to call me if they're not happy, and yet I'm as lonely as the Old Maytag Repairman?" and then we concluded with, "Watch my free video at…" and then we give the website. This is a lead generation device sending them to content on this product, which is a management and customer service product. This is an example of an information product or information lead generation magnet.

And then, of course, there's my favorite lead generation magnet. It's one I've been using with 3D Mail since 2009. It's a free book offer, and it has worked very well for us. I've sent over 15,000 of these books to prospects.

Here's a handful of examples of lead generation magnets that can be used for the sole purpose of generating leads for your business. A lot of you would have probably seen this first one. That's the Columbia House CD/DVD/cassette, going all the way back to records of the Month club. What you

32

see here is "Would you believe? 13 records or tapes for just one dollar." That was an amazing, irresistible offer on the front end. And then, that morphed, of course, into "8 CDs or 12 cassettes" over the years. And then, "12 hot hits for a cool penny." As you can see, they really developed this over the years, and did very well with it.

Now that we've gotten that out of the way, let's dive into the five battle-tested strategies to create the most compelling offers for your product or service to help you achieve the most success with direct mail and ultimately make more sales.

Next, we're going to discuss your Unique Selling Proposition, guarantees, testimonials, and credibility, using deadlines with your offer, and then I'll finally wrap it all up with some tips for crafting a compelling offer.

Unique Selling Proposition

We're going to start with the Unique Selling Proposition. You'll see as we move forward how a well thought out and well worded Unique Selling Proposition can be the basis for an entire irresistible offer and even an entire business or an entire industry.

Here is a definition of a Unique Selling Proposition that I love. I haven't been able to find one better than this. It's from my mentor, Dan Kennedy, who says, **"Why should I, your prospect, do business with you versus any and every other option available to me in your category?"**

 Dan Kennedy is referred to as the "Professor of Harsh Reality" for his bluntness. But his marketing and sales acumen is off the charts! To receive $633.91 of free money-making marketing and sales information from Dan Kennedy and GKIC go to Kennedy.3DMailResults.com

This is the most important and probably the most challenging question you'll ever answer about your business. It's designed to be concise and differentiate you from all other competitors. This is the starting point for just about any offer you will create. Let's go over a few examples, and then we'll go over how you can craft one. Let me give you a notable example, one of the all-time best:

There are two kids and they want to work their way through college. They need more money than a regular job will pay. Their family has no money and they have no scholarships. They took over a failing business on the edge of campus for no money down. While one kid is going to school by day, the other is working in the business at night. They'd switch every semester and take turns. But the business kept losing money.

One of them bails out but the other one stays and invented a ten-word USP that changed everything. In fact, it made him wealthy and changed an entire industry. Are you ready for it?

"Fresh, hot pizza delivered in 30 minutes or it's free."

34

Now, notice there was nothing said about good pizza, nothing said that it was the freshest ingredients or anything like that. All it did was guarantee fresh, hot pizza in 30 minutes or less.

That's what we're talking about. That's the kind of power the right kind of USP can have. In this example, not only did it create an irresistible offer - which is pizza in 30 minutes or less - but it also created the business, and it really revolutionized the industry. That's the power that a Unique Selling Proposition can have. Let's dive into a couple of other examples, and then we'll show you how you can craft a Unique Selling Proposition for your business.

You don't need to have a USP that revolutionizes a business or an industry. Here's an example from Chauncey Hutter, Jr. He took over a $50,000 a year tax business, and quickly turned it into a $4 million a year business. How did he do that? By changing his thinking about the business through a Unique Selling Proposition. He got out of the 'tax preparation business' and into the 'free-money-fast business.' So, this USP completely changed the direction of how he advertised and how he made offers. His USP became **"The biggest and fastest tax refund loans allowed by the IRS, guaranteed."** Nothing spectacular, nothing world-changing, this didn't change the CPA and tax preparers industry by any means, but it changed Chauncey's business.

Now, instead of being in the business of tax preparation he got into the 'money now' business, which is a great business to be in. Here's an example of one of Chauncey's ads.

How do you find your Unique Selling Proposition, how do you craft it? This is very rarely something you can pay somebody else to do. You can certainly get a consultant or a coach to help you do this or a mastermind group to help walk you through this and help you get some ideas. But, ultimately, the best USPs I've ever seen almost always come from the business owner or a team of employees. What are some of the ways you can find your Unique Selling Proposition?

36

First is price; if you simply have a better price than everybody else. Frankly, this is not a place I like to live. If you study business history, you'll see that typically the price leaders in any given industry may not quickly burn out, but they almost all eventually burn out. So, the gold standard of the price USP right now would be Walmart, and before that it was Kmart —and we all know what happened to Kmart. Before that, it was somebody else, and, in fact, they're gone. I don't even know who to give you an example of; Woolworth's, I guess. If you have a price that is better than everybody else, it can work. Oftentimes, this can be for a singular product to get them to buy other products or services.

I shared the Columbia House example earlier. They had that irresistible offer of eight CDs or 12 records for a dollar. That got them in the door with the great price, but the thing that we all figured out down the line was: we ended up having to buy a whole bunch more cassettes, records, or CDs at full price. We bought at a low price, but they eventually sold us things that were of industry-normal prices or higher! I would caution you on using price as your USP. You may want to use it simply on the front end to get clients or prospects into the door, and then have other products or services on the back-end that can make up for the low margins.

Next is a product that is simply different than anyone else's. Quite frankly, it doesn't have to be a product change, it can be a change in thinking like it was for Chauncey Hutter. The end game for Chauncey, before his USP and after the USP, was the same, which was a completed tax return. The product remained the same, but the avenue in which he advertised it was different. The product went from being tax-return service to being "cash-quick." He switched how he presented and sold the product. He had the same product all along, but he just changed how he phrased it, changed how he advertised it.

37

Another way to find your USP is if you have a process that is different than anyone else. Those who studied advertising know about Ivory Soap™ and their 99.8% pure soap used in their advertising. Well, to be honest, most soap is 99.7% pure, but because they used it in their advertising they were able to give themselves a leg-up for decades on many other soap producers.

There was a time, about 80 to 100 years ago, that Schlitz Beer™ was the gold standard in American brewing. It wasn't Anheuser-Busch™, it wasn't Coors™, it wasn't Miller™, it was Schlitz™. And the biggest reason they became the largest brewery in the country was that when they did their advertising they touted the process of how they brewed their beer.

If you go back and look at those ads, they were brewing the beer the same way as everybody else. However, they were the only ones to put out advertising and marketing that told people how the process was done, which then lifted them up in the minds of consumers. Whether real or imagined, the process you have can also do that. If you have a service that no one else can provide, that's another source for your USP.

And lastly, your marketing. Is your marketing substantially different? Here's another quote from my mentor, Dan Kennedy, **"He who can spend the most money on advertising and marketing to get a client is going to win, because if they can spend the most, that means they're typically charging the most."** If you can separate yourself in the way that you market and advertise to your prospects and clients, you can find a UPS in that regard as well.

Here are some questions to ask yourself, as you're creating your USP:

- What do you **DO** better than anyone else in your category?
- What **CAN** you do better than anyone else in your category?
- What **SHOULD** you do better than anyone else in your category?

Those are three questions to ask yourself as you're going through and trying to create and craft your Unique Selling Proposition.

Here's a great USP, one that touches on all three of these questions:

WHAT IF YOU ACTUALLY
LIKED YOUR ATTORNEY?
- We Listen. - We Respond.
We Return Your Phone Call.
Life is Frustrating Enough...
Your Attorney Shouldn't Be.

How is that for USP? That ticks off all those questions:

- What do you do better?
- What can you do better?
- What should you do better?

I call this a competency USP; by providing a competent service, you have elevated yourself from all your competition. I absolutely love this USP.

Here's a good way to test your current USP or the one that you come up with after a few months: Can your employees tell you your Unique Selling Proposition? And, more importantly, can your clients tell you your Unique Selling Proposition?

Creating your USP is going to take time. The first time you sit down, you're not going to hammer out a USP. I encourage you to take time and think about it. Get your employees involved, get outside help if needed. Somebody from the outside isn't going to be able to create it for you; you're going to have to do the heavy lifting.

Ask your clients: I've found that clients may even reveal a good USP when you speak to them. They may tell you the things that you do well. They may not be able to create the entire USP for you, but you can take bits and pieces of it, and build from there. What do they say they like about you? What do they tell you they like about your business? That's one way to craft a very compelling Unique Selling Proposition.

Guarantees

Next, we're going to talk about guarantees. My thought with a guarantee is: if you can't guarantee it, don't sell it. That's my credo. If I can't guarantee something, I'm not going to sell it.

There are three kinds of guarantees: There's a **satisfaction guarantee**, which says, "If under any circumstances you don't like..." So, all they've got to do is not like the product, the service, whatever, for any reason and you're going to give them their money back.

Next is the **results guarantee**, "If after 12 months you're not growing bigger, brighter tulips..." That's a results guarantee.

And lastly, the third kind of guarantee is the **perception guarantee**, "If you don't feel this was the most valuable event..." Those are the three main kinds of guarantees. We're going to go into examples of each type of guarantee shortly.

Before we get into the specific examples of those three kinds of guarantees, I want to give you a little copywriting tip. It matters how your guarantees are worded and named. If you simply say, "satisfaction guarantee," or "your money back guarantee," that's okay, but frankly, it's rather dull and ordinary. You can make a satisfaction guarantee sound much more interesting and exciting, and you should.

People perk up and play close attention to the guarantee, so it's a fantastic opportunity to sell, not just state a policy. Here's what I mean; how the Pearl Cream business (whose figurehead was Nancy Kwan) did theirs. They said, "If your friends don't accuse you of having a face lift, return the empty jar, and we'll give you all your money back." Now, isn't that much better than saying, "Money back guaranteed" or "Satisfaction guaranteed?" That is so much better, it adds to the copy, it adds to any advertisement or marketing that you're going to do.

Here's one I wrote for a client, a motivational speaker for corporations and colleges. We called this the "You'll be a star guarantee." We stated, "If you don't think that my show was the most amazing you have ever seen, and people are not coming up to you after the show, patting you on the back for having such a magnificent event, then you don't pay a dime, guaranteed."

Again, how much better is that than simply stating, "I offer a money back guarantee?" Which would you rather be presented with? Which do you think is boring? How you word it is vitally important, and how you title it can be vitally important too.

Multiple guarantees almost always outperform a single guarantee. Here's an example of a multiple guarantee that I use when I offer the 3D Mail Direct Marketing System (www.3DMailSuccess.com). I state, "If you are not delighted with your results or unhappy in any way whatsoever, simply return the System within the first year, and I'll return all your money." That's a satisfaction guarantee. Again, the way we worded it makes it better, as opposed to just saying, "100% money back guarantee." I'll go into detail of what that means later.

Now, we add to that with a multiple guarantee. We offer a "Double your money back guarantee" which says, "Use any of the letters in the 3D Mail System as the basis for your letter to your prospect or client, call your client a year later, and ask them if they remember your mailing. If they don't remember it, I'll give you double your money back."

As you can see here, we have a double guarantee. We have our regular, one-year, no questions asked satisfaction guarantee. And then we double it by giving them 24-months, followed by a result-based guarantee. We tell them if they call their client and they don't remember it, we'll give them double their money back. This is a great way to amplify your existing guarantee, to add a second guarantee behind it. It usually needs to be some sort of guaranteed results.

There are often stipulations when offering a results-based guarantee like this. When I wrote this "double your money back guarantee" I explained that you must show us the letter that you mailed and you must give me the name of the person you called. Quite frankly, I'm probably not going to call that person. If I think the client is being a little sketchy, I might. But if it's a someone I trust, and he truly didn't like his results, and he truly did this, I'm going to give him double his money back. I can tell you from experience that this guarantee almost always gets more sales than if I do it just with the single guarantee.

Next, there are **unconditional** versus **conditional** guarantees. Unconditional guarantees are just that, unconditional. They are under no obligation to meet certain parameters or conditions. They simply get their money back, no questions asked.

Conditional guarantees are the exact opposite. Your client must do something to get the guarantee. In my double guarantee I'm using an unconditional and a conditional guarantee. My suggestion is to always have an unconditional no questions asked money back guarantee, but then add to it with a conditional guarantee.

Before we move on, let's look at two more guarantees that you can use —these are the two that I have used very successfully. Here's an example of a **satisfaction based unconditional guarantee**, and it says:

"You can see everything for free with this one year, no-risk 100% money back guarantee. However, if you do ask for a refund, and you think for any reason that I have wasted your time, simply let me know, and I will add another $100 from my own pocket just for your trouble."

Here's one that is a result based, conditional guarantee that was used along with the previous guarantee.

"If after two years you haven't made at least $10,000 extra, just show me that you've done something, and I'll give you all your money back, guaranteed."

That's an example of a conditional guarantee used in conjunction with an unconditional guarantee. Think about how you can use guarantees in your business, and you can make them work to create irresistible offers.

Testimonials and Credibility

Next on the list is **testimonials** and **credibility**. Quite frankly, these two topics are really underused, and they can be some of the most powerful selling tools you have at your disposal, especially when creating the kind of irresistible offers that I'm talking about. There are many forms of testimonials and credibility, and I'm going to touch on a lot of these, but the most powerful are proof statements that are in the form of a well-crafted testimonials from your customers, clients, patients, or members.

"What your customers say about you is 1,000 times more persuasive than what you can say about you, even if you are 1,000 times more articulate and eloquent."

That's the power of testimonials. People are drawn to them, they overcome skepticism, it's really a powerful way to craft an irresistible offer, and really put the odds in your favor.

We're not talking about the quantity of testimonials, but the quality of the testimonials. Quantity is good, having a lot of them is good, but if given a choice I would rather have fewer quality testimonials versus a whole lot of just "okay" testimonials.

Here's what we're talking about when it comes to quality testimonials:

- We want meaningful specifics
- We want actual outcomes
- We want them to overcome objections
- We want them to reinforce benefits,
- We want them to be emotional.

It's very rare you're going to get one testimonial that covers all five of those, however, you want to have as many in each category as possible.

 One of the best ways to get amazing testimonials is to have a team dedicated to exceptional customer service. Our Sister Company, Keith Lee Business Systems, has an amazing training system on customer service. Visit www. TheHappyCustomerHandBook. com to get a free book on delivering amazing customer service.

Here's the deal with testimonials: You need to have their full name and other details. Never use them blind. I'll show you an example of that here, but in many cases, you'll want to use the person's full name. If it's in the B2B world, you'll want to use the business name. If applicable, you may want to use the person's occupation, the number of years they've been a client or patient, the city and the state where they reside, and any other pertinent information that you think would be meaningful to your prospects who are going to read those testimonials.

I hate to be harsh, but the truth of the matter is that most testimonials are simply trash. This is typically what you'll see, "You're really great, and the service was as expected — John D."

What does that tell you? Does that do anything? Does that move the reader or listener? Does that do anything at all to convince somebody that your business, your product, your service is the way to go? All too often, this is exactly what you see.

Here's an example of a great testimonial. This is one we have for our former business, American Retail Supply. Pay attention to the words and the things that she mentioned are overcome:

"We are a hospital gift shop in rural Western Montana, staffed and managed by volunteers. Recently, we purchased Smart Register™, and after six weeks there is no way we could go back to the 'old way.' Training for the volunteers with many different computer skill levels was so easy. Our rep from the first days of planning to opening the shop up to the present is Mark Turner. He is a treasure. It doesn't matter what I need, it only takes a call to Mark, and he makes it happen. He explained the Smart Register and demonstrated it for us at the California Gift Show in July, and we started using it full-time in the shop mid-October. Thanks for everything. Alice Balbi, Manager, Mementos Gift Shop, Clark Fork Valley Hospital in Plains, Montana."

Now, that's a testimonial that is a terrific addition to an irresistible offer. There are the specifics: from the very beginning, Mark was her sales rep, and that we started with them in July. There are the outcomes: "after six weeks, there is no way we could go back to the 'old way.'" It overcame objections: "Training for the volunteers with many different computer skill levels was so easy." It has direct benefits, and you can just feel the emotion in Alice's choice of words. And then, obviously, the full contact information.

Now, Alice Balbi will not be the manager of Mementos Gift Shop forever. However, we can use this testimonial for a very long time because it gives the name of the business, it gives the location, and when Alice does leave, and somebody says, "Boy, I really want to find out if American Retail Supply is telling me truth. I can call Mementos Gift Shop, and say, "Hey, do you guys have a Smart Register System?" And, if they still have our system and are happy with

46

it, they should have no problem telling that person that they love it.

I've had that happen. I've given lots of testimonials that are true; I don't make them up. I've given lots of testimonials to people over the years, and occasionally people will get on the phone and look me up, call me, and ask if I really said that. It doesn't happen all the time. It's maybe happened three or four times since 2008, but that's the perception that you want to give your reader. That if I was looking for a point-of-sales computer system I could reach out to Alice Balbi at Mementos Gift Shop in the Clark Fork Valley Hospital in Plains, Montana. I could find that person with a very easy Google search, and track them down. That's the kind of assurances you want to give your reader when it comes to testimonials.

Testimonials can be broken down into three types: The first is an **Outcome testimonial**. This is just like it sounds, it has a before and after vibe to it. One thing I will say is, be careful with outcome testimonials. The FCC has cracked down on testimonial usages in a lot of industries since 2010. So, if you're in the money-making world, weight loss, health & wellness, financial world, and others, just be on the lookout; make sure you have a good business attorney to speak with about using testimonials. Having said that, you can use testimonials. You can use outcome testimonials, and I'm going to show you how.

There are **service, quality, and perception testimonials**. And then, there are **testimonials that overcome an objection**. Those are the three kinds. And we're going to look at each different one here.

Here's an outcome testimonial:

"The carpets look so amazing! They've never been softer! I never walked around my house barefoot before, but now I do all the time just to feel it on my toes!"

That's one I made up but notice the emotion inside and notice the specifics. It's not just that the carpets look great, we give them an outcome, which is, "We walk around barefoot now." Compare that to, "The carpets look great, and they're clean." Compare them. How much more emotion, how much better is this and how much more believable is this?

Here's a service/quality/perception testimonial:

"Thank you for your wonderful service and products. I'm a first-time customer, and all your staff were excellent on the phone. I received follow-up phone calls to make sure I received the catalog I'd requested. I'm very happy to do business with you. Thank you again!"

You'll notice there's no before and after, there's no, "Here's what happened before, here was the change, and here's what happens after." This is simply speaking to the quality and the service that we provided. Again, these are all just examples and I would include the name, city, state, occupation and all the other things I mentioned earlier.

And then, the last one is how you can overcome objections. Here's one we've used in the past, this is a real one; I omitted the name, but it says:

"I thought for sure using 3D Mail was cheesy and not professional enough for my business. However, all my doubts were erased when I saw the results of my first 3D Mail campaign."

This is an overcoming an objection. You can see in the second sentence we cross over into an outcome testimonial, and this could serve dual purpose as an overcoming of an objection and an outcome testimonial.

What if you're just starting out and you don't have testimonials? What if you neglected collecting testimonials over the years? The first thing to do is to have a user group to manufacture testimonials. What you should do is give away the product for free or very inexpensively in exchange for a real, honest testimonial feedback. This is great for two reasons: One, you'll uncover some holes in your product or service, and they'll be happy to tell you. Two, if it's a high-quality product or service, you'll have a ton of testimonials to start off with.

You can also use industry endorsements of a respected expert. Now, I'll be honest with you, when we started 3D Mail we didn't have testimonials, especially outcome-based testimonials, because we had just started. It's hard to have outcome-based testimonials when you don't have any outcomes to show people. How did we overcome this? We went and found books, articles, magazine articles, etc. We went and found respected people in the industry who had used dimensional or 3D mail; people like Dan Kennedy, Jay Abraham, and Gary Halbert. We found passages from books and articles, and then we would reference those. In Dan Kennedy's case, he had many quotes on using dimensional mail in his various books. We took passages out of the book or article and referenced them, and then told the reader exactly where to find them. So, it wasn't a testimonial for us or our service, but it was a testimonial for the strategy, for the idea that we are selling.

Another way to do it is to retool them from another product/service you may provide. Again, this is exactly what we did when we started 3D Mail. 3D Mail was built on the back of a business called American Retail Supply; a business we owned at the time. We have all kinds of testimonials that make no mention of the business but make mention of the quality of service that they received; how the phones are answered within a certain number of rings, and they're answered live, not by an automated recording, that packages are shipped out quickly. We felt perfectly comfortable using those types of service/quality/perception guarantees, because, quite frankly, there wasn't any question in our mind they would be transferable to the new business. The phones were still answered the same way, the packages were still shipped out the same way, you still had access to a team member if you had any issues at all.

The last way is to retool them from one niche to another. Perfect example of a client of mine, who is a painter. He's been a painter for many, many years, exterior and interior. Over the years, he's added many services. He's added power washing services, he's added handyman services, things like that. And with each service, he certainly didn't have any testimonials for that new service, but what he did was he moved the testimonials from the painting over into those worlds where they would work. And again, these were mainly the quality, the service, the perception testimonials that he used. Because, again, he didn't have any outcome testimonials yet, because he didn't have any for those products or services, but he retooled them, and made them work in another part of his business.

How do you get great testimonials? Well, the first one should be obvious: have delighted customers. That should go without saying, but if you provide a quality product, if you provide a quality service, the testimonials will naturally come. Now, they may trickle in, they may not come as quickly as you maybe want them to or would expect them to, but if you're in business for any amount of time, and you have happy clients, they will just naturally come. If you don't have delighted customers or happy clients or happy members, that's a real problem, and that's going to be something that we can't fix in this book. But, if you have thrilled customers, they should naturally come in without you doing much, to be perfectly honest. But there are ways to stimulate them.

First, be greedy. Tell your customers what you want when asking for them. Not only tell them that you want them, tell them the type of testimonials you're looking for. Are you looking for outcome testimonials or are you looking for objection testimonials? Tell them. This is a wonderful thing to have in place in a first order follow-up sequence, when you're going to put them in a campaign, and you're going to ask them for testimonials as part of that campaign. You can be very specific here. But, be greedy, tell them you want them, tell them you'd like to hear from them.

About a week after someone's first order, we send out a simple email that says:

Subject: "Good or bad, I want to know."

Dear Tommy, this is Travis with 3D Mail, and I just want to know if everything turned out okay with your order. Good, bad, or indifferent, please let me know."

We get a lot of people that reply to that email. Most of them are just okay, they're the ones that we talked about that aren't very good or very specific. But occasionally you'll get a great testimonial that you don't need to do any editing with, you don't need to prod or provoke them to do anything more, they'll just give them to you. And then it's just a question of asking them permission to use it. Simply tell your customers what you want.

Next, here's one I use quite often, and it's really overlooked. Help your customers write them or write it for them and proceed to get permission to use them. I'm not talking about putting words in their mouth. I'm not talking about writing something out of the blue, and then emailing them and asking them to use it.

This is typically what happens when we use it: I'm at an event, or I'm out speaking, and I'm talking with the people afterwards. Invariably, there's always somebody there who's used our stuff with great success. Oftentimes, those people will seek me out, and they'll say, "Travis, I've got to tell you about our results," or, "Travis, I've got to tell you about the service I got." Oftentimes, there's no way to capture their story right there. What I'll do is I'll make a note that simply says, "Rehash Johnny's story."

Then, I'll come back to the office, and write essentially what Johnny had told me. Then, I send that to Johnny and say, "Hey Johnny, when we met at this event you had told me some of your impressive results. This is what I remember you saying. Do you mind if I put your name to this and use it in my marketing?" And I'll tell you what, I've probably done that a few dozen times, and not once has anybody told me "NO," not a single time.

As you're talking to your clients keep your antenna up, really listen to what they're saying, listen for the things that they're thanking you for, put it on paper and then ask them to use it. It's really that simple.

Lastly, when it comes to getting great testimonials, it's all about timing. I could go on and on just talking about timing on testimonials and when to ask for them, but as a big general rule of thumb you want to ask for that testimonial when the person is at their happiest, when they are the most satisfied with your product or service, and that's usually right after the product or service has been delivered.

For the carpet cleaner it's immediately after the buyer steps on their carpet and feels it for the first time. For a retailer, it's at the cash register, after they've paid, gotten their garments, and said, "Thank you, I really appreciate that." That's when you can then go into a script that you may have to ask for a testimonial. For us, we've found that it's right after they get their order, when we either ship it to them or mail it for them. It is at that point that they're the most jacked up and happiest about it. That's when we ask for a testimonial.

I've assigned a considerable number of pages discussing about testimonials specifically, but there are other forms of credibility, that I just want to touch on here, so that you know that they're out there, and so you can use them. First are any awards you've won. That may or may not be obvious to you. I'll give you an example from my painter friend I told you about earlier in this book. He had been voted the "Best of Kent," which is a large city south of Seattle. He was voted best painter in Kent, not one time, not two times, but four times in a row. And it took him until the third year to realize, "Hey, maybe we should put that little 'Best of' logo on everything that we do." So, it's on his trucks, it's on his vans, it's in his advertisements, things like that. So, don't overlook those things. Anything you've won, a community award, an award from your industry, use those things. They add credibility.

Next are articles you've written and where they've been published. You can have case studies, white papers, books written about you, all those types of things are great. And then, of course, pictures or videos, before and after pictures, bank statements, checks, all kinds of stuff, these are all diverse ways that we can get credibility without having testimonials.

Lastly on testimonials, I hear it all the time, "Travis, I can't use testimonials in my industry. I can't use these ideas. There's no way I can do this." I hear it all the time, especially in certain industries. First off, they're usually just plain wrong. There usually is no rule, no by-law, no ethical standard of using testimonials. What they are confusing themselves with are outcome testimonials. So, in many places, you cannot use outcome testimonials, but that still gives you the range and the freedom to use the other kinds of testimonials that we've discussed. If you're in the finance world or weight loss or health & wellness or money making, you might get your hands slapped or worse by the FCC for using outcome testimonials. However, almost all other kinds of testimonials that we've talked about are free to use.

I'll give you an example. Remember the lead generation magnet I shared with you from Ryan Cole, who wrote the book for LGBT investors in New York City? Well, he's a financial advisor, he cannot use outcome testimonials; he cannot say, "Betty's gotten 12% return year-over-year for 30 years, and I can do the same for you." He cannot do that. So, we use other kinds of testimonials. We used lead generation marketing for them to request the book to raise their hand. Well, we can put all the testimonials we want in that sales letter about the book that we're offering, and we make no outcome guarantees. It doesn't make any guarantees about money made or anything like that. All it simply says is that the book was great. It says it more eloquently than that, as we discussed. But that's how we get around it in the financial world.

Let's say you're in the health & wellness world. You obviously can't use outcome testimonials that say, "Doctor Smith cured me of cancer." You certainly can't do that, and I wouldn't expect you to. But you can use testimonials of perception or of quality. Let's say Doctor Smith did magnificent work for John Doe. He can certainly use John's testimonial as, "Every time I came into Doctor Smith's office the nurses and the reception people were so comforting and so warm, and the best thing about it was Dr. Smith was never late for a single appointment. He always sees me at the exact time he says he will."

We talked about the competency USP with the lawyer. Remember that, way back at the beginning of this chapter? They had the competency USP of, "We care, we'll call you back." Well, she's not going to use a testimonial that says, "John, the lawyer, got me off murder charges." You don't do that. But we can certainly use the same kind of testimonials we use for the doctor we just gave. So, perception or service testimonials are on the table for most businesses. Just because you've been told you can't use testimonials doesn't mean you shouldn't find ways around it. Really investigate it. It's very likely you can't use the outcome testimonials we talked about, but you can certainly use the other kinds of testimonials that we've talked about.

Deadlines

Let's move on to tip number four, and that's using deadlines with your offer. To be frank, if you don't have a deadline with an offer, you don't have a direct response ad, and thus you don't really have an irresistible offer. Deadlines are vital with any direct response and direct mail campaign. They are what makes direct response marketing what it is. It's truly what separates direct response marketing from mainstream Madison Avenue brand-building advertising.

Here's why we use them: the fear of loss. Deadlines create a fear of loss and they create urgency. People are motivated by fear of loss. We do things like: response required within "X" numbers of days or by a certain date. I went out and bought a date stamper with bright, red, bold ink, that reads "expires on," and then we can spin the dial, and put the date on it. We'll use that stamp at the top of a letter we're sending out. So, by a date stamped in red on your letter. Limited to the first "X" numbers or just a limited supply. These are all ways to create urgency and to create a deadline for your offer.

And here's a biggie: don't hide your deadlines! These aren't things to be hidden away in size four invisible ink. I'm sure you've all been in this situation, where you've tried to redeem a coupon and only be told that it expired, and then you look in the itty-bitty fine print. I had this happen to me at a sandwich shop not too long ago. I had a collection of these coupons, dollar off this, free chips with that, that kind of stuff. And I've been collecting them for a while, and I've been using them. I'd gone like a month or two without using one, so I pulled one out, and it was expired. There is nothing worse than thinking you're going to get a discount and then not receiving it because they hid the deadline. You want them to know the deadline, and in fact "deadline" should be big and bold. You want them to know the deadline, because it increases response. Don't hide them, get them out there.

Multiple deadlines often work with a reward or bonus for fast response. Here's an example of one that I love: "This offer expires in four weeks, but if you respond in two weeks you'll also get..." You'll often see this with a specific offer, and then they add a gift to it if you respond before X date, or they give another kind of free bonus if you respond quicker. That's an incredibly effective way to create deadlines and create urgency for your irresistible offer.

Lastly, some general tips and tricks for crafting a compelling offer. The first thing you need to remember is that your prospect or client or patient is constantly tuned in to their favorite radio station W.I.I.F.M., "What's in it for me?" Your client is not interested in what you're selling, and I know that's hard to take sometimes. We all think that we have the greatest product or service in the world, or else we probably wouldn't be offering it. But, they're just not that interested. What they are interested in is the results of what you're selling and what it does for them at a personal and emotional level. So, get away from features; that's really what the bottom line is here. Get away from features and turn them into benefits. If your barbecue cooks at a higher temperature than every other barbecue out there, tell them the benefit of that, not the feature. Always tune into their favorite radio station, W.I.I.F.M.

Next, should you use a discount, should you use a premium, or should you do both? Here's what we mean by a premium. A premium or a gift is often used in conjunction with something you want them to do. Here's an example: the financial planner will buy you a free steak dinner if you meet with him for 45 minutes. It may be a premium or a gift with the purchase and not even an appointment. And I'll tell you what: "free" is still a very powerful word. Perhaps you discount, maybe you don't, but if you can somehow slip "free" into your offer somewhere, that's extremely powerful.

The guys who are very good at this are the direct response television guys, the Ron Popeil's of the world, the Billy Mays' of the world. They'll often give you an amazing discount and a gift. Well, they wouldn't go to all that trouble to give away that free stuff if it didn't work. Those guys test and measure everything. I'm not saying you need to go out and make an infomercial for your product, but look at the offers they make. See how they bundle them. See how they put them together; you'd be wise to mimic them in any way that you can.

 Download our free catalog of the 49 Low Cost & Powerful Premiums/Free Gifts to Explode Your Results & PROFITS at www.3dmailresults.com/gifts.pdf

In thinking about discounts and premiums, you can often boost conversion with a premium alone. The premium or gift will cost you less than the discount. You may give away a free steak dinner or a free report or a free unrelated item. Vanity items often out-pull practical or informative items. Remember the *Sports Illustrated*™ Sneaker Phone? That's a perfect example of an unrelated vanity gift.

Giving them multiple choices is better, so if you can give them, "Pick any two of the three listed below," or "Pick one of the three." If you can add the choice, you now go from, "Do I want 'X'" to, "Which of 'X,' 'Y,' and 'Z' do I want?" That's very, very important.

Another consideration; should you have a basic and a deluxe version of anything that you offer? Again, it's kind of like the premium, where you go from, "Do I want 'X,' yes or no?" to, "Do I want 'X,' 'Y,' or 'Z,' which do I want?" That's a big psychological change. But if you give them a choice, as far as what the product offering is, a basic and a deluxe versus just "no" you're going to dramatically increase the response of your ad.

And here's an advanced tip. If you add the option of a basic and deluxe option, you'll see that more and more people might start taking your deluxe. As a big general rule of thumb, when you start to get 65% of the people taking the deluxe option, offer the best option. Now you have basic, deluxe, and best, and now you've got three different options. Who knows? You may completely stop offering the basic version as you move forward.

When you're creating your offer, there should be a logical reason for the offer. We all know there's no such thing as a free lunch, and we're often skeptical and suspicious. We've often used things like "new to the neighborhood" mailers or "anniversary sales," or "our vendors are helping us" sales. We don't want to just have a sale for the sake of having a sale, or just have an offer for the sake of having an offer. We want to have a good reason for it. I gave you the example of Ryan Cole and his LGBT book. We mailed that out with darn good success, not too long after the Supreme Court ruled that gay marriage was now legal throughout the country. We were quick to capitalize on that. That was the reason for the free book offer. If you can tie it into current events, all the better. I'll be honest with you, we kind of had some fortuitous timing with that, we happened to be thinking about dropping it, and then the news came, and we scrambled to add it to it. You always want to have a reason for the offer. Tell them why they're getting this irresistible offer.

Remember, people are interested in themselves, how your offer benefits them. Not the features of your offer, but how it benefits them. The end results.

CHAPTER 3

Direct Mail Success Secret #3: Choosing The Right 3D Mail (creative) Item For Your Campaign

Welcome to the final chapter of this book. I congratulate and thank you for getting this far.

In this chapter you're going to see actual mailings and letters that our clients use and their results. This isn't theory. This isn't stuff that we <u>think</u> is going to work. This is stuff that we <u>know</u> works and that's the difference between this and most books. Unlike others who work in theory and classrooms, this is tested. This is something that has worked. I'm going to show you the exact pieces that were mailed, go as in-depth as possible on all of them, and you're really going to see the power of what 3D mail can do for your business.

Whenever I go out speaking, particularly to a live audience, I always ask, "How many marketing messages does the average American see in one day?" It turns out that most people say a number way too low. Occasionally, I get somebody who goes bonkers and gives a number that they know isn't real.

The average American sees 3,800 marketing messages per day. That may seem impossible but think about your day. Think about the moment that alarm goes off in the morning and you turn on the radio. How many advertisers do you hear when you turn on the television? How many commercials are you seeing? How many ad placements or product placements are you seeing on television shows? Even on the news. Those fancy Microsoft laptops are placed there for a reason!

Furthermore, let's say you get in your car and you drive to work, how many Golden Arches signs do you see down the road? That's a marketing message. How many little sandwich boards do you see sitting outside on a sidewalk telling you about the daily lunch special? That's a marketing message. Here's a biggie. How many e-mails do you get every single day? As you can imagine, the 3,800 adds up very quickly.

And it's not getting any better. Here's an excerpt from Dr. Samuel Johnson in his essay "The Art of Advertising Exemplified," **in 1759:**

"Advertisements are now so numerous that they are very negligently perused. It is therefore becoming necessary to gain attention by magnificence of promises, and by eloquence; sometimes sublime and sometimes pathetic."

I love this picture of Times Square in New York (next page). I wish I would have taken the picture myself, but I did not. If you look around, almost everything you see is a marketing message; everything from the billboards to the ads on the taxis and the buses, even the fare schedule on the taxi is an advertising message, plus all the signs, all the bright lights, just about everything in this image is an advertisement!

If you take 3,800 and multiply that by 365 days a year, the average American is going to see just under 1.4 million marketing messages per year. So, the question becomes how to break through all that clutter. If you were to walk down a portion of Times Square and you were to try to take in every advertising message that you see, it would take you days, weeks or even months to walk down the street. You'd be looking at everything. We have trained ourselves to "put blinders on." If you can picture in your mind's eye the blinders that a race horse wears so they can't see their competition on the left or the right - anything to spook them or give them pause - that's what we've done. We have literally put on blinders over our ears, over our eyes, and we just focus on the things right in front of us.

The real challenge now has become how we break through these blinders for our marketing message to be seen, heard, or read. There are a couple of simple ways we can do this. The first way is to advertise on the Super Bowl™. The reason Super Bowl ads are so expensive is because you are guaranteed eyeballs. It is guaranteed that people will listen and watch. And not only that, the Super Bowl™, for a lot of people, has become about the ads and the TV commercials, NOT the football. That is a sure-fire way to get noticed. If you've got an extra $4.5 million lying around, which is what the average cost for Super Bowl™ advertising has been over the last two seasons, then you go ahead and do that.

My guess is there's not very many people who have an extra $4.5 million to throw at a Super Bowl commercial.

Therefore, it's wise to opt for the next option, *The Big Bang Theory,* which is one of the most watched network television shows today. At the beginning of 2017 it had the highest cost for a commercial, which was just over $300,000. More of a *Walking Dead* kind of guy or gal? It's the most watched "non-live" TV event each week, and that will cost you around $400,000. Neither are quite as good as the Super Bowl because you're not going to get as many eyes. Many people are going to skip the commercials if they record it on their DVR, it but if you've got an extra $300,000-$400,000 lying around, you too can advertise during *The Big Bang Theory* and the *Walking Dead* and very likely, you're seen, heard, or read.

Realistically, that's not feasible for most people reading this book. Getting seen, heard, or read is the number one hurdle for any kind of marketing. It really doesn't matter if you're doing yellow pages or billboards or outbound telemarketing or television commercials or direct mail. It doesn't. The biggest hurdle we have is being seen, heard, or read... Getting attention. My question to you is, "How can you stand out?" How can you be remembered as the one in nearly 1.4 million marketing messages your prospect or client is going to see each year? My promise to you is before you're through reading this, you'll know how to be a 1 in 1,387,000 marketers of your business. You will be the one that gets remembered after you see some of the examples in this chapter.

What's the first thing people do when they get home? They check their mail. 92% of people in the U.S. check their mail every single day. 86% open it the day that they get it. Direct mail is still alive and well and it's not going anywhere anytime soon. And contrary to what most people think, people enjoy receiving direct mail. In a recent study by the *Direct Marketing Association,* it was shown that even millennials like receiving direct mail more than other forms of marketing. Direct mail is alive and well. It's not going anywhere.

 If You Are Frustrated and Dissatisfied With the Results You're Getting From Your Direct Mail Advertising, Then The 3D Mail Direct Marketing System is For You! Visit www.3DMailSuccess.com

Here's the challenge: Direct mail obviously has its own set of clutter. Those of you who get a decent amount of mail can relate to this. I want to get into what we call the "A-Pile." There are three categories of mail. There's "A-Pile," there's "B-Pile," and "C-Pile." These are terms coined by Gary Halbert. Gary Halbert passed away not too long ago. For the modern direct mail copywriter and strategist, he is the "IT" Guy (www.thegaryhalbertletter.com).

So, what's in the C-Pile? It's the obvious junk mail that you know you don't want. It looks like everything else you receive every day. As you can imagine, this usually goes right into the trash can, right into the recycle bin, sometimes unopened and oftentimes not looked at, simply discarded right away, never to be seen again.

What's in the B-Pile? This what I call mail purgatory. It's stuff you might be interested in. Let's say you get a *Valpak*™ or *Money-Mailer*™, you might not check them immediately but will do so later. In our neighborhood our homeowners' association has a little mini magazine flyer that they send out and that goes into my B-Pile. Other things like magazines and the water bill are the types of things that end up in the B-Pile. We all have a place where we keep this stuff in mail purgatory. Sometimes, we read it. Sometimes we don't, but at least it sticks around for a little bit longer.

What then is A-Pile mail? A-Pile mail is mail you open and read immediately, oftentimes without delay. What kind of message ends up in there? Test results from your doctor! This is an example I like to give. It's a little extreme but at least it illustrates a perfect picture in your mind. Let's say you're having some health issues and you go to your doctor and he does a myriad of tests on you. One of the things they do is draw your blood. He says, "Travis, we're going to send the blood sample off to ABC Laboratories. They're way over on the East Coast and in about a week or two you're going to get the results in the mail whether you're healthy or whether you're not."

A week goes by and you walk out to the mailbox and you see test results enclosed from ABC Laboratories, the place that did your bloodwork. Are you going to wait to open that mail? Is that going to go in the B-Pile? No. It's certainly not going to go in the C-Pile either. In fact, you may open that letter right next to the mailbox or right next to wherever you receive your mail every single day. This holds true for both B2B (marketing to other businesses) and B2C (marketing directly to consumers) which will be later discussed in this chapter.

What else ends up in the A-Pile? Letters from grandma; Grandma still sends letters. Grandma still writes them by hand and sends them in the mail and she doesn't use e-mail. That ends up in the A-Pile. And from what we found through our extensive testing and our 7,500 different clients who have used this since 2007, 3D Mail also ends up in the A-Pile.

For clarity sake, I think it's important to briefly explain what 3D Mail is. It's mail that has length, width, and depth. Normal mail is flat. If you consider all the mail that you get in your mailbox, most of them lie flat. Most of it is a number 10 envelope for a credit card or a postcard for the local gym or a postcard for a free appetizer at the local restaurant. If you've been around the direct mail world for a while, you may have also heard 3D Mail called lumpy mail or dimensional mail. It all means the same thing. I call it 3D Mail, three-dimensional mail.

Within 3D Mail, there are two categories. First, we have grabbers and enclosures. A grabber or enclosure is an envelope with something inside of it. Here's an example of a mailing we did for Rusty Prewet who's a client of ours. He's an insurance agent and he sent his clients who didn't have auto insurance a little toy car. That's a great example of a grabber.

Here's another example, a little shamrock for a St. Patrick's Day Campaign from our long-time client Jeff Giagnocavo, Owner of Gardner's Mattress and More in Lancaster, PA.

The second category is what is called self-mailing 3D mail items. These are things like a real vinyl bank bag. This enables you to put your letter inside the bag; you put your postage on the outside, you put your mailing label on the outside and you mail your bank bag just like what is indicated in the picture below.

The bottom line is it looks different from everything else in your mailbox and stands out from the clutter of 1.4 million messages that we see every year. That's our number one hurdle and if we can overcome that number one hurdle, getting noticed, we've done the bulk of our job as a direct marketer.

Why would you as a small business owner want to use 3D Mail?

I will get to specific reasons shortly, but first off, it's endorsed by some of the top copywriters and direct marketing strategists in the country. Dan Kennedy, a long-time client and mentor not only uses my packages all the time, he recommends it to his company, GKIC (www.GKIC.com), and to many of his private consulting clients. He says,

"The use of object-mail & grabbers plays a role in almost every direct-mail campaign I develop for my private clients as well as for my own use. Travis Lee at 3D Mail Results is my go-to guy for these items and for fresh ideas. I have brought in Travis and his team for projects, referred clients to him, and turn to him time and again for the right items at the

right price. You'd be foolish not to use 3D Mail Results as your preferred resource as I do."

A lot of people are familiar with Bill Glazer who is Dan's former business partner. He has since sold his stake in that company and is now a very sought-after marketing strategist and consultant. He was kind enough to say:

*"All of my clients know that not only do I like 3D Mail a lot, but I use them a lot. It's because I want my mailing to have a better response, and that's exactly what 3D Mail does. 3D Mail does a lot of great things, but the biggest thing it does, which is the only thing our members should even be paying attention to is, it increases response. **The return on your investment will be much, much higher than the cost, it almost always pays for itself."***

There are more testimonials like these that show the efficiency and credibility of what I do. In fact, it's been used for decades upon decades in direct mail. The strategy itself is nothing new but it overcomes the biggest hurdle we face in direct mail. Any message that isn't opened can't be acted upon. I have yet to see a business owner send a piece of direct mail and say, "Travis, I sent out 10,000 pieces. Nobody opened it and we had a positive return on our investment." It just doesn't happen. If your message doesn't get opened and read, it cannot be acted upon no matter what it is.

Because of this your mail must be on top of the pile. If you send something like the trash can or a message in a bottle or just about anything else that we offer, it must be the first thing on top of the stack. If the stack doesn't stack, it can't be a stack. It ensures your message is going to be on top. That may not seem like a big deal, but if you're the first thing people see in their big stack of mail, that's a huge leg up in your favor. They're going to spend the most time with your message. Anybody who is familiar with direct mail knows that the more time we can get them to touch, hold, and feel our message, the better.

One thing I caution is not to get carried away in the false belief that, "my business is different." Many of my clients who sell to other businesses say, "Yeah, Travis, this may work great. This may work great for consumers who aren't all that sophisticated, but this doesn't work for me." On the flip side, I have businesses who market to consumers who say, "Yeah, that's fine. That may work for other businesses but there's no way that'll work for me, I market to consumers. I don't market to other businesses." Don't fall into that trap.

Let me relay a personal experience to lay credence to that claim. This whole business started because of another business my father and I previously owned and grew. It's a company called American Retail Supply (www.AmericanRetailSupply.com). We grew that first business using these same kind of direct mail concepts. That business sold (and still sells to) "mom-and-pop" retail stores on Main Street, to huge retail stores doing hundreds of millions of dollars per year, and everything in between. This works in the B2B world and it works in the B2C world. What you need is an open mind and to make sure that you're receptive to new ideas. I'm going to show you examples from both worlds in different industries. You can see for yourself that this works.

Let's talk about the Elephant in the Room. Many people want to know if 3D Mail is going to cost them more than "regular" mail. It's is often true, but not always. Many 3D Mail campaigns cost less than printing a fancy flyer. Cost isn't even the real issue. All we're really concerned about is the ROI, the return on investment. If I send out 10,000 postcards for 50 cents apiece but don't get any response, that's wasted money. But instead, I send a smaller, more laser-targeted list using our 3D Mail and get 5 to 20 responses, it's infinitely better than doing cheap things that don't work.

My recommendation has always been that you start with a smaller, laser targeted list and send multiple mailings. You'll get better results versus the shotgun mailings I just described. Also, remember to send only to a segment of your list. When I do mailings, whether it's a new client or a new prospect mailing, these are people who don't necessarily know me. In fact, I never send to everybody on a complete list. I break them up into segments, test and measure, repeat, test and measure, repeat. You just need to test it. Pick something and start small. As you look at some of these examples, think of how you can test this and have an open mind. How can you convert it from business 'A' and make it work in your business? Remember, the number one goal through all of this is to cut through the clutter and get attention.

The first example comes from Dr. Greg Nielsen. Dr. Nielsen is a chiropractor in Waterford, Wisconsin. It's a small town about 40 miles outside of Milwaukee. It's farm county. It's not a huge town. He sent this mail to a lead generated list. These are people who have raised their hand and said, "Yeah, Dr. Nielsen. I'm interested in your practice," but they haven't become a patient yet. That's what I mean by a lead generated list. It's not a red-hot list but it's a warm list.

The Doctor used our Message in a Bottle. These messages in a bottle are self-mailers. The mailing label is put on the outside as well as the postage. Something critical to mention with these messages in a bottle is they open from the bottom. I recommend you

70

replicate what the Doctor has done. He handwrote "twist to open" on the mailing labels. Simply stick the bottom edge of the mailing label over the opening to ensure it stays closed. It's not going to pop open in its route to your prospects or client's mailbox. Then, the Doc rolled his sales letter, tucked it into the bottle, put the bottom of the cap on and placed his mailing label on the bottle. To see a video of this process, visit www.3DMailResults.com/product/message-in-a-bottle

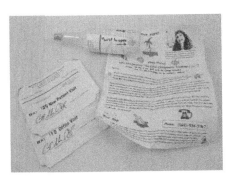

One thing I love that he included is the "new patient" slip. As a chiropractor he used two little prescription pads, see the image to the left. One of them was for a $25 new patient visit. The other one was designed to be given to somebody else by the recipient, a referral. The referral also gets a $25 new patient visit.

Dr. Greg Nielsen consistently gets 25-30% response rate sending out 200-300 per month. There's a caveat however; he didn't start out sending that many. He didn't just say, "We're going to send out 300 a month and see what happens." He was smart about it. He tested it. In fact, I think his very first order with us with the Messages in a Bottle was 48 and it did well.

He e-mailed me after the package worked out well for him and said:

*"The bottle, by far, has generated the most response of any mailer I've done. **We make $2,055 for every $100 invested in this promotion** and that buys some serious grilled cheese sandwiches for the family."*

Imagine someone who sits at home or in the office and receives a Message in a Bottle; he's surely going to open it.

The next example is Blake Walker at Central Avenue Automotive in Kent, Washington. He's my mechanic whom I met when I was having some issues with an older car of mine. Coincidentally, he learned about my work immediately gave it a try.

Blake Walker targeted his 1900 inactive or lost clients. These were people who had brought one of their vehicles in and had not been in again for 1-3 years. He sent them a Boomerang, because "he wanted them back," (Get it? We want you back?). An example of his letter is on the next page.

"Travis, We
Want You Back!"

Dear Travis,

It's John and Jason over at Central Avenue Automotive in Kent. We were reviewing our records of all our great and loyal past customers the other day and we noticed that it's been quite a while since you had your vehicle in, **we really miss you**. In fact, the last time we saw you was January 13, 2012. It's been too long!!

That's why I've sent you this boomerang, **because we really want to see you back here at Central Avenue Automotive!**

We talked it over and we thought we'd give you the best prices of the year on any service or repair your vehicle needs. We can't keep these prices forever so these "We Want You Back" special prices **expire on Feb. 28th**. Check them out:

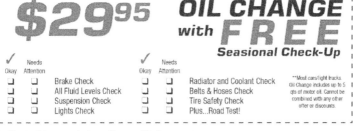

At Central Avenue Automotive you'll always get:

» **Honesty & Integrity:** We will never suggest a service for your vehicle that is unnecessary.

» **Quality & Value:** We offer the best products and services at the best value.

OVER, PLEASE

» **Safety & Dependability:** We take your family's safety seriously, as if it were our own. Our skilled technicians will keep your vehicle on the road and running like new.

We will constantly strive to offer and deliver incomparable automotive service and repair, with exceptional customer service to you and your family that will meet or exceed your expectations.

We offer a 3 year/36,000 mile warranty on all of our parts and labor, giving you the peace of mind you need to get behind the wheel of your vehicle.

We really do want you back, give us a call today!

John and Jason
Service Managers, Central Avenue Automotive

P.S. <first>, we can't keep these prices forever so these "We Want You Back" special prices expire on Feb. 28th. **Call today, 253-854-6762 and make your appointment before these prices expire**

Call us before Feb. 28th 253-854-6762

1514 Central Ave S. • Kent, WA 98032
Schedule Your appointment: 253-854-6762
We Service All Makes and Models

Blake followed my tried and true, "fill-in-the-blank" formula in his letter which I have used for dozens of different campaigns. It's the simple headline of, "Travis, we want you back!" I encourage you to read the entire letter. It's "boiler plate" copy that anybody can use. Blake, to his credit, has done a lot of marketing and therefore knew that this was a good offer to make. For best results, I included a map with his shop and other pertinent information like website, phone number, e-mail, and the like.

Here are Blake's amazing results.

- Mailed 1,881 boomerangs
- Total cost of $2,131.50
- Reactivated 51 clients
- The total revenue $24,275 the first time back
- Average Transaction $475.98
- **$11.38 to $1 return on sales**

Let's assume he has a 50% cost of goods to deliver his services. He's still at 5.5:1 return on his investment. A lost client campaign is something that any business can do.

I told you that Blake's letter was created using a fill-in-the-blank template that we provide. I want to reiterate that fact with another client in a completely different business. This is Tim Mitchum who's a sales rep at Wexford & James in West Des Moines, Iowa. He's in the receivables management services (a.k.a. a bill collector). You know, when you can't get people to pay your bills, you send people like Tim and he goes and breaks ankles and busts down doors to get your money. It's a little bit subtler than that, but that's the industry that Tim is in.

Tim, in the B2B realm, uses the same letter template as Blake. I got an e-mail from Tim which reads,

"Hey, Travis. Just thought I would quickly share some results from the Boomerang mailing we did earlier this year. So far,

it has returned 1,200% and I expect that to go a little bit more. Will have to do another mailing of some kind to that same list. Thanks."

Here is Tim's letter:

"We Really Want You Back!"

Dear [first name],

Our records indicate it's been too long since we've heard from you at <<your company>>. So, we're giving you the *Flat 10%* <<your company>>*Gift Certificate* in this letter. Meaning any file less than 1 year of age that you send to us for collections, received prior to March 1ˢᵗ, will be at a *Flat 10%* contingent rate fee. "*No minimum balance required*. We will help you with any size file."

Here are 5 Reasons Why Our Competition Hates Us But You're Going to Love Us...

1) **You Get to work with an Integrity driven company who believes in full transparency.**
   (Here's an example:
   Wexford is 100% contingent based, meaning you pay nothing unless we collect money. You will also have access to view REAL-TIME activity, notes, and resolution information pertaining to your accounts with our WebAccess software.)

2) **You Get HIGHLY experienced collectors working for you.**
   (Here's an example: Wexford's collectors have an average of 15 years experience in the collection industry. Meaning, they are skilled at finding creative solutions to help the debtor pay the debt without ruining the client relationship.)

3) **You Get A company flexible to your needs:**
   (Here's an example: Wexford is large enough to handle your volume, but nimble enough to be flexible to meet the needs of your systems for reporting and other requirements.)

4) **You Get free continuing education to help you improve your in-house collection efforts.**
   (Every month you will receive value added information designed to help you become even more effective at your in-house collection efforts.)

5) **You Get 3 SUPER easy ways to place files for collection.**
   1. Email file to placements@wexfordjames.com
   2. Fax to Lisa 515-369-7075
   3. Website www.wexfordjames.com and click on place an account.

HURRY! Offer Expires March 1ˢᵗ!

Sincerely,

Tim Mitchum
Wexford & James
VP Business Development

P.S. Hurry and call today so we can reconnect! We really do miss you!
P.P.S. This gift certificate for a *Flat 10% Rate* expires March 1ˢᵗ, 2012. Call me today!

Here's the last lost client I'm going to share. I want to share how easily transferrable this idea is to ANY business. This is Dr. Lenny and Nancy Anglis, who own the practice in Indiana. They sent a worry doll to patients who had cancelled their consultations or did not proceed with the prescribed work after the consultation. This is an "appointment-no-sale" letter. If you have appointments that people missed or if you have consultations or meetings and you want them to purchase or you have appointments that don't result in immediate sales, whatever the business is, be it an insurance agency or a dental clinic like Dr. Leonard's, this is a perfect campaign you can use. Here it is:

We Are Worried
About YOU!

Dear <<FIRST>>,

Yes, we are worried about you. My office manager, Kim, checked on your consultation appointment that was canceled and not re-scheduled. You contacted us because you need us to evaluate your smile, and something urgent must have come up in your schedule to cause you to cancel this very important appointment.

We understand how busy your life is, and we are happy to re-schedule for another complimentary consultation at this time. All of us have tended to neglect ourselves as we are busy taking care of others and their issues. We do know; however, that when we are at our best, we can do more for other people! Being at our best means having a healthy smile, and you can achieve the "smile of your dreams" with us!

Remember: At this complimentary smile masterpiece consultation, we are going to answer all of your questions in a friendly, open manner, and we are going to provide you with a number of choices to correct any problems you are experiencing now.

The most important thing for you to do was to call and schedule the appointment, and you did that so we know you want to move forward with your consultation. Give us the opportunity to meet with you, and to pamper you in one of our luxury tropical resorts. You will truly enjoy your time with us, and you will gain a full understanding of what is happening inside your mouth at this time.

Until November 15, 2013, we will have a special gift waiting for
you upon your arrival to the consultation appointment.
One call to 1-877-526-4547, and we will take care of the rest!

We look forward to meeting with you!

Dr. Leonard F. Anglis, DDS, MAGD, ABGD, ABID and Team

P.S. These little worry dolls originated in Guatemala, and parents with small children would place them under their pillows at night so all worries would stay with the doll. Sometimes, the parents would take them away before morning to signify that the worries were gone. We want to take all your "dental worries" away, too!

There is nothing world-beating here, it's very formulaic. They used a proven template for the worry doll, "We Are Worried About You." Len and Nancy kept it very simple. They attached the worry doll to the upper right-hand corner of the letter and used a handwritten font for the address on a #10 envelope. It does not get any easier than this.

Most business completely under-value their Lost and Inactive Cutomers. For a comprehensive, FREE Training on how to profit by targeting your Inactive customers visit Lost.3DMailResults.com

Here are the results which I really couldn't believe when she emailed me. They mailed 530 of their customers with a total cost of $1,100. The total revenue was over $101,300 on the first visit back. This doesn't include follow-up visits, referrals, and so on. That's what's so cool about marketing to your lost or inactive clients or patients. The return on this campaign is 85:1. I've always maintained, there's nothing earth-shattering about this other than the fact that the Doctor and Nancy were proactive.

Here's the actual e-mail I received from Nancy sent to me on Nov. 11, 2015.

Gentlemen,

We could hardly wait to tell you that we just had our most successful mailing utilizing your unique worry dolls! We crafted a letter and featured your worry dolls and mailed it to 530 patients in our dental implant practice at a cost of $1,188.33 - including all supplies and labor.

Our astounding results have produced $101,300 in dental treatment to date! And we are expecting that figure to further increase next week with scheduled appointments! Wow! We hope to get into your "record books" with this one!!!

Many thanks,
Len and Nancy Anglis

Nancy reported to me several weeks later at a conference we both attended that the number was approaching $120,000 or $140,000.

We've spent a lot of this section in the consumer world. Let's look at a few B2B examples.

This next example is another boomerang mailer, but this is different than the boomerang lost client mailers we talked about before. This is from Jimmy Nicholas and he owns Jimmy Marketing in Waterford, Connecticut. You can see him at jimmymarketing.com. He does online marketing, web design, social media, and video. Jimmy sent the boomerang mailer but not for lost clients, if you will, but to get them to immediately come back for an upsell to a different service he provides. This is commonly referred to as a "bounce-back" offer, as we want the client to "bounce-back" for a second purchase.

There are numerous assorted products or services that he offers and once he sells product A, he wants you to buy products B, C, D, and F as complementary or cross-selling products. He used the boomerang to do that. In fact, I'm going to share Jimmy's experience because he was kind enough to talk to me extensively when I met him a couple of months ago. Here are excerpts from what he discussed with me. To watch the entire video and to see Jimmy's actual letter, visit jimmy.3DMailResults.com.

"I'm the owner of jimmymarketing.com. We're a local marketing company out of Waterford, Connecticut, and I recently did a boomerang mailing, not to get my customers that haven't done business with us, but to get them into our membership program where they renew every month automatically. It's a subscription product. I also wanted to get them back in for other services instead of just their subscription program. I thought why not send them a boomerang to get them to come back in. The headline is taken directly from Travis's swipe file, "Dear name, we really want you to come back," and did some copy doodles with "we miss you" and I did four different offers for them to come back. It was a one-page mailing and that was it. (editor: to see Jimmy's actual letter visit jimmy.3dmailresults.com)

We sent out 243 letters and we had eight responses, seven of which turned into actual closed business for approximately a 3% response rate. The postage cost me $473.80. We sent that in a clear bag with the boomerangs, I didn't even know you could send mail in a clear bag until I got on the phone with Travis and asked, "What do we send this in?" and he suggested, "Why don't you send it in a clear bag, so they see the boomerang?"

I can tell you that It's just tremendous. That was $22.64. The paper and ink were $25.47, and the boomerangs were $50.94 for a total cost of $572.90. It brought in over $4,826 of revenue which is a return on investment of 742.38%. This was my first 3D mailing I had ever done and it was extremely successful. We're still getting orders in from it and it's been about a month. We put an expiration date on it. We're still taking some of them in, but it has been a tremendous investment. I have nothing but wonderful things to say about 3D Mail."

That is a splendid example of Jimmy finding a campaign that worked in one business and making it work in his. He used it as a cross-sell opportunity. He used the same idea of getting them to come back but he changed up the offer a little bit. He changed up the timing significantly and made it work.

Let's continue with the business-to-business theme with another example. This comes from Tim Mitchum. He did the lost client campaign with the boomerang as you probably remember. Tim has done quite a few other projects with us; this one targeted cold prospects. Remember, he's in the bill collecting business.

He targeted just 30 cosmetology schools in Iowa and three surrounding states, a very small, targeted list. These aren't enormous numbers. Tim does well with cosmetology schools and he knows that. For whatever reason, they have a need for bill collectors which he acknowledged and consequently aimed for the low-hanging fruit. He targeted just 30 of them in and around this area and he got a 3,300% return on that $200 investment within the first three months of the campaign.

You might be thinking, "Golly, a $200 investment for 30 mailers. What does that turn out to be?" Just a tick over $6 each. Why would anybody want to send a $6 mailing to somebody? Well, as I indicated earlier, it doesn't really matter what the cost is if your returns are greater than the cost and you can make money at that rate. With the 3,300% return, I am certain that Tim is making money on that. In fact, he's told me as much. Plus, he can expect an ever-increasing lifetime return because these people are going to be constantly giving him money. Within three months, his return was 3,300% but bear in mind that every month, these new clients will send him business and then if they give them referrals, it just snowballs from there. As you can imagine, getting these new clients is very valuable.

82

Here's the first page of Tim's letter. Along with the letter he included a little foam foot because he "Wanted to get his foot in the door." This is one of the cleverest ideas I've ever seen:

"How To Recover More Past Due Student Tuition While Maintaining Your School's Good Name"

And finally get a handle on the process so it's simple, effective, and super easy to implement....

Dear Leo,

I'm guessing you probably don't receive little squishy feet in the mail very often. Well, let me explain. I did that for three reasons:

1. To grab your attention
2. Add humor to your day (we all need that)
3. To see if now is a good time for Wexford to get our "REAL" foot in the door to help St. Charles Barber College.

You have worked hard to provide a quality education that prepares students to go out into the world of cosmetology and make a great living doing something they love. A living that provides great joy to those they serve. The education you provide gives them the ability to change a person's whole perception of themselves which could change someone's life. It's a big deal.

But The Truth is...Running A Cosmetology School Is Anything But Easy.

And if you are like most I talk with you care deeply about your student's success. You see them every day, you know the struggles they are going through at any given moment, and you most likely know a lot about their family and upbringing. You celebrate their successes and provide a caring ear when they are struggling. You are invested in them as a person, as much as a student.

When Everything Goes Perfect You Have A Student Who Comes To School, Graduates, Gets A Job, And Pays Off The Loans That Helped Them Get There.

But sometimes, as you know, that doesn't necessarily happen exactly like that. And then you are forced to make a decision that is hard, especially when you are so invested in your student's success. You have to decide when to utilize an outside agency to help them resolve the debt they have that is either financed by you, or reflects on your schools ability to get funding.

OVER,
PLEASE ↓

As I said, Tim is a sales rep for Wexford & James and **so his job is to get his foot in the door.** He just wants an introduction and time, whether it be face time, or virtual face time, or time over the phone, so he sent a little rubber foot. The foot is about four inches long by four inches high.

83

In this next example, I will venture back into the consumer world, it comes from Stuart Spencer. He owns Advanced Ear Care in Laguna Woods, CA (www.advancedearcare.com), a retail store that sells hearing aids. For this campaign he hosted a weekend event for his clients and prospects. Here's Stuart.

"My name is Stuart Spencer. I own Advanced Ear Care, Laguna Woods, California, and we just did the promotion with the treasure chest provided by Travis and his team. We put a letter in the treasure chest with some little goodies inside the treasure chest but when we mailed it, it was locked so they had to bring the treasure chest in for us to open it up and they revealed a discount towards a purchase. It was an upgrade thing for our hearing aids. We had a fantastic promotion. We're going to be about $80,000 in sales just off that one mailing. Travis, thank you very much."

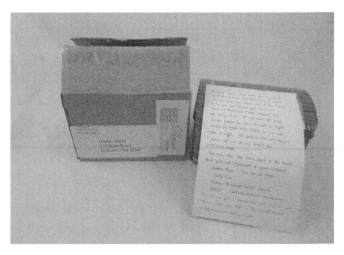

He hosted a weekend event for his clients and prospects. This is a client appreciation event where he had the parking lot full of games, barbecues, and the like. He invited his clients and he invited prospects who had come in but didn't buy. We call this "event-based marketing." He sent out the treasure chest to his past clients and his unconverted leads and they did just over $80,000 in one weekend from the treasure chest.

The cool thing about this treasure chest is that it comes in a box. You take the treasure chest out, fold up your letter, stick it inside and then you stick the whole package back inside of the box, tape the box shut, and you use that as your mailing package.

He sent the little treasure chest locked with a note on the top (see image on previous page). The letter read, "You're cordially invited to the Laguna Ear Care customer appreciation. Inside this treasure chest is a gift for you. I'm the only one with the key. When you bring this locked treasure chest to the event, I'll unlock it and we'll reveal your prize."

Everyone who received a treasure chest had a winning ticket inside ranging from a $5 gift card to a real nice dinner to even a new TV which was the grand prize. They had to bring this whole package in to Stuart at his retail location during the event, get him to unlock it and reveal the prize. It's a cool way to drive people to your retail location if you have a storefront. A financial advisor, an insurance agent, an auto repair shop, or anyone who wants to drive traffic via direct mail to their retails storefront could use this.

There are two more examples I would like to share. The next one comes from a friend of mine, a long-time client. His name is Steve Clark and he's with newschoolselling.com. Steve Clark is a sales trainer based in the Florida panhandle. Here's what he did. It is called an "endorsed mailing" or "partner marketing mailer." He and a coach in the insurance world were targeting insurance agents and financial advisors. They wanted them to come to a sales training seminar hosted by Steve. However, they all had a relationship with this "host" coach who was coaching the agents and advisors.

They were invited to a $97 seminar. A first letter was sent by the "host coach" telling them to be on the lookout for a mailing from his friend, Steve Clark. Steve's mailing went out in a bank bag. The bank bag is our most popular piece. It's the piece that people use regularly and more often than any other piece.

With the bank bag, you put your mailing label on the outside with the addressee's name. You put your postage on the upper right-hand corner, zip the bag shut and drop it in the mail. It's that simple. The reaction you're going to get from your prospect or client or patient when they see this show up in the mailbox is crazy! It must get opened! Here's what Steve had to say (visit 3DMailResults.com/product/bank-bag to see Steve's video case study):

"I'm Steve Clark, the CEO of New School Selling. We've worked with 3D Mail Results and after about four years, we've done several mailings. We recently did one in which we did the bank bag for the second time and it was even more effective than the first time. In fact, we've got an $18 return for every dollar that we invested in doing the mailing with the bank bag and every time we do something with them, it produces multiple return on our investment."

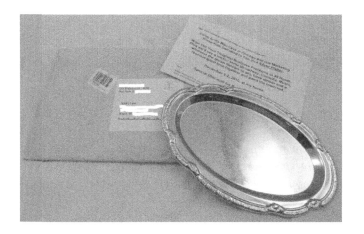

Here's my last example and it comes from a good friend of mine and a long-time client, Walter Bageron from Power Control Services in Broussard, Louisiana. Walter has since sold the business for millions of dollars; however, you can still see the business at www.powercontrolservices.com. One of the reasons he could sell the business was because of the direct mail techniques I taught him. He fixed, repaired, and refurbished power and electrical systems, circuit boards, LCD displays, motor controls, inverters, touchscreen displays, etc.

His target audience is Electrical engineers, Mechanical engineers, Computer engineers, and people you would think of as being uptight, stuffy, and not having a good sense of humor. However, Walter made a smart move and mailed out a silver platter mailer.

The platter is 6" x 9". He used the headline: "Here's an opportunity so important, it needed to be delivered on a silver platter." Here's a quick little story of how he used it and what it meant for him and his business (visit Walter.3DMailResults.com to watch Walter's video case study):

"My name is Walter Bageron of Power Control System in Louisiana. I want to tell you all the success I've had with these guys. I've used their products many times and it's part of what helped me become marketer of the year and earn the EXTRA $1.1 million when I sold my business. One of the successes we had is with their silver platter. I'm in industrial sales. We are not in a sexy business. This is not something that people jump out and say, "Yeah, that's what I want to do," but the great news about that is that when we use something unique like these 3D pieces, it makes an enormous difference in our income.

"The silver platter stands out like you wouldn't believe. People do not expect to see this in their mailbox, especially from an industrial sales guy. The letters that these guys provide to me make me look like the hero because it seems I'm a great copywriter, but I'm not. I just put my name on it, steal their products and send it to my clients and money comes in the mail. It's something I love doing and I've used quite a few of their products, too. The silver platter works fantastic for us."

Would You Like Me To Personally Double, Triple, or Even Quadruple Your Business... For Free?

Dear Friend,

I'm looking for a great client that I can bring in massive results for. If you're that client, I will personally work with you one-on-one in your business to help you double, triple, or maybe even quadruple your revenue for the next 12 months.

You Pay Nothing Out of Pocket

Here's why.

The first thing I'm going to do for you is to personally help you create a strategic plan to bring in immediate money. **I call this my "Breakout Success Session."** There's no charge for this and it only takes about 45-90 minutes of time together.

I'll even do most of the heavily lifting for you.... telling you exactly what to package and how to position your offer for ongoing sales and profits. At the end of this initial planning session one of these three things will happen:

1. You love the plan and decide to implement it on your own. If this is the case, I'll wish you the best of luck and ask that you keep in touch with me to let me know how you're doing.

2. You love the plan and ask to become my client, so I can personally help you execute, profit, even implement it for you right away. If that's the case, we'll get you some amazing results... And that's a promise.

3. In the unlikely and unprecedented event that you feel like you wasted your time, I will send you $500.00 as payment immediately. No questions asked. Your time is your most valuable asset you have, and I respect that.

It really is that simple and there's no catch.

Think about this. The "worst" that can happen is you get $500 for "wasting" 45-90 minutes of your time. The best that can happen is we work together one-on-one to increase sales and profits several times over.

That's Why This Is the Closest Thing To FREE MONEY You'll Ever See

Here's how it'll work:

First, we get on the phone one-on-one (yes, with **ME** personally) and go over your business. I look at what you've got, what you're doing, and what you want to achieve going forward. Once we have that foundation, I help you come up with a strategic plan of action to immediately increase your profits dramatically.

There are many ways I might do this for you. For example, I might show you:

- ➢ How to **restructure your offer for a better price point**
- ➢ How to create **recurring revenue**
- ➢ How to **pull in buyers from untapped sources**
- ➢ Or how to **reactivate past customers**

And if you have a list of prospects, we're bound to whip up a promotion you can run within days... and have the sales flowing in repeatedly. And like I said, there's no charge for this.

So Why Would I Offer It?

Two reasons:

First, I enjoy it. This type of thing is what I do best, and it makes me very, very happy to see someone **achieve financial success** (and all that comes with it) because of the help I give them.

Second, it's how I attract top-level clients. Here's how that works:

Assuming **you're happy and you want me to crank out these types of plans for you all the time**, you'll probably want to continue working together long-term, so I can help you. You may ask for some help and guidance through the process, to "keep your feet to the flames," if you catch my drift.

Or, it may mean I create a specific direct mail piece for you (you are using direct mail, or else you wouldn't have received this offer), or build a follow-up program for your unconverted leads, <u>or just plain implement the ideas we come up with for you.</u> **Simply getting your marketing and advertising ideas out to your market can be <u>90% of the battle</u>.** And I can help you do that, too.

The "fee" is $997 a month... but if you think about it, **it really doesn't "cost" you anything.**

Why?

Because I expect to make you much more than $997 in the first month (try around $10,000 more each month) ... and if we keep working together I'm confident I can double your entire business... at minimum. Many of our clients see as much as a 3x increase in their business within the first 12 months.

But look. If you don't want to become a client, don't worry about it. I honestly don't mind one way or another – you can take the plan and implement it yourself, you can get my help with it, or you can walk away entirely, $500 richer for the time you invested.

In fact, here's <u>my promise to you:</u>

You Find Our Conversation To Be Incredibly Valuable Or I'll Pay You $500.00 Immediately To Compensate You For Your Time.

Now, obviously this is an amazing offer.

Think about it.

I'm personally generating a profit-plan for you up front - for free - and then letting you pay me later if (and only if) you decide to work together long-term. Plus, I'm taking it one BOLD step further by guaranteeing you'll find this free plan immensely valuable - **or I'll pay you $500.00** just for wasting your time. Just tell me, and it's yours. No questions asked.

Who Else Would Do That?

NOBODY (I checked).

But I'm happy to put it on the line like this because I know that if we spend the time together, you're going to get value. **My strategies work, and I know that if we work together, you'll make money.**

Anyway - as you can imagine, I'll get a LOT of interest from this letter. And that's why I need you to read this next part carefully:

This Is _NOT_ For Everybody.
Here's Who I CAN Help:

I'm VERY picky about who I'll speak with and I've got a strict (but reasonable) set of criteria that needs to be met for us to proceed. Here it is:

1. You must have a solid business already. This offer is for people who are up and running already and simply want to run a lot faster and a lot farther. And I won't work with beginners or people bringing in less than six figures in revenue yearly.

2. You must have a steady flow of leads and customers. This means that you're getting consistent traffic, web visits, inquires, and making sales already. It's probably not where you want it to be, but you've started and you're making money. You don't have

to be "everywhere" or "huge" ...I just need you to be PRESENT in your market.

3. You must have a list. It doesn't really need to be that big... just responsive.

4. You must have a good, solid product and a good reputation. Everything we do together will not only bring you more sales and profits, but we'll be doing it in a way that creates MASSIVE goodwill in your market. For us to do that, you need to have your act together. You need to be an entrepreneur who has built up a business because of YOUR passion.

5. You MUST follow directions. (Don't worry, I won't ask you to do anything crazy.) After all, if you don't implement the stuff I give you, neither one of us will make money.

That's it! Those are all my requirements.

Here's What I Want You To Do Next

If you meet the criteria above and would like to talk to me personally about getting you incredible results, then I'll happily set aside some time for you. <u>Here's how the process works</u>:

First, you'll need to fill out an application. Don't worry, it's simple and unobtrusive. **I just need to know what you're selling and get an idea of what you want to accomplish.**

I'm also going to ask for a "real person deposit" of $250. Don't worry, I could care less about your $250. I'm just using it as a "filter" to keep the time-vampires at bay. **I'll give it**

back right after we hang up (unless I take you as a client - and in that case, I can apply it to your balance).

Here's What Will Happen After That

Once I have your "real person deposit" and your application, Tara from my office will call you within 48 business hours and set up a time for us to talk.

Our initial call will last about 20 minutes. Based on your Application I'll have a few questions for you, and I'm sure you'll have a few questions for me. I want to ensure, 100%, that I can help you get what you need.

The truth is, I don't have magic powers and I can't help everybody, and I don't want to waste anybody's time. But in the very high likelihood that we're a match we'll schedule **our "Breakout Success Session" right then.**

The Breakout Success Session will be between 45 and 90 minutes. This is where we really begin working to figure out exactly what you want **...and how to make it happen.** I'll painstakingly review your goals, your offers, and so forth... **and I'll deliver a plan to bring in money immediately.**

If you see the value in becoming high level client, great! We can talk about it.

And if you don't want to become a client - that's OK too. I'll return your deposit as soon as we hang up. No biggie. And if you tell me I've wasted your time, I'll give you DOUBLE your deposit back immediately. <u>So, you literally can't lose.</u>

(By the way - I've never had anyone feel like their time was wasted. EVER. That's why I can make this offer. I DELIVER. Would anyone else take such a risk?)

WARNING - TIME IS A FACTOR

This opportunity is extremely limited because of the intense one-on-one time needed to provide you with results. Therefore, it is physically impossible for me to work with more than a handful of people.

Also, you should realize there's a very large demand for personal one-on-one help from me, **and what I'm offering to you is unprecedented**.

With that said, know that the window of opportunity won't be open long. If you feel like this is right for you, **please visit Meet.3DMailResults.com** and complete the online version of the "Breakout Success Session" Application.

Made in the USA
Monee, IL
19 July 2023

39599822R00063